PREDESTINATION AND OUR WILL

The Bible's Astonishing
and Wonderful Teaching

Predestination and Our Will

The Bible's Astonishing and Wonderful Teaching

Douglas Daudelin

Word Of Grace And Truth
P.O. Box 325, Allamuchy, NJ 07820-0325

Predestination and Our Will: The Bible's Astonishing and Wonderful Teaching

Copyright © 2025 by Douglas Daudelin

Published by Word Of Grace And Truth, P.O. Box 325, Allamuchy, NJ 07820-0325

All rights reserved.

Unless otherwise indicated, Scripture quotations are taken from the New King James Version®. Copyright © 1982 by Thomas Nelson. Used by permission. All rights reserved.

Scripture quotations marked (NASB) are taken from the (NASB®) New American Standard Bible®, Copyright © 1960, 1971, 1977, 1995 by The Lockman Foundation. Used by permission. All rights reserved. www.lockman.org

Scripture quotations marked (LITV) are taken from the Literal Translation of the Holy Bible. Copyright © 1976–2000 by Jay P. Green, Sr. Used by permission of the copyright holder.

Scripture quotations marked (YLT) are taken from the 1898 Young's Literal Translation of the Holy Bible, public domain.

All Scripture quotations are shown in italics, and all bolded emphases in them have been added by the author.

Cover design: Anna Daudelin

ISBN: 979-8-9867423-2-8

To my children and grandchildren,

that you may arise and declare these things to your children,
that the generation to come, those who will yet be born, may know
that it is our God who reigns in the heavens above and in the earth beneath,
and that these matters may not be a cause of stumbling to them,
but inspire them to seek the Lord and His blessing,
and serve Him with joy and trembling.

Contents

    Preface 9

1 Introduction 11

2 Our Will 15
    2.1 Definitions 16
    2.2 Its Use in the Bible 18
    2.3 Our Willing Choices 18

3 What Influences Our Will 21
    3.1 Ordinary Deliberation and Persuasion 21
    3.2 Faith and Repentance 22
    3.3 How We Have Been Made and Molded 23
    3.4 Adam's Sin 24
    3.5 Being Enticed by Our Lusts 25
    3.6 Spirits 26
    3.7 God Turning a Heart 27
    3.8 God Giving Restraint 29
    3.9 Hardening One's Own Heart 30
    3.10 God Hardening One's Heart 30
    3.11 God's Direct Influence 31
    3.12 God Giving a New Heart 32

4 Can We Choose Our Will? 33

5 We Are Responsible for Our Willing Choices 35

6 Our Choices Make a Difference 39

7 We Choose, but God Determines What Happens 43

| 8 | When Does or Did God Ordain Events? | 49 |

9	The Paradox	53
9.1	God Has Predestined	53
9.2	We Make Real Choices	53
9.3	How Both Can Be True	55
9.4	How God Can Foreknow Our Choices	60

10	How Ordained Events Come to Pass	63
10.1	Natural versus Supernatural Means	63
10.2	God's Natural Wonders	66
10.3	God's Required Intervention	67

| 11 | Salvation and Predestination | 69 |

12	Why Did God Make Us Differ?	73
12.1	Did He Not Make All Differences?	76
12.2	Some Say He Did Not	77

| 13 | Why Did God Create All Things? | 79 |

14	God Is Not Evil	83
14.1	Why Then Did God Ordain Evil?	83
14.2	God Never Does What Is Morally Evil	87
14.3	God Does Not Share in the Evil of Our Sins	88
14.4	God Does Not Tempt Us to Sin	89
14.5	God Justly Finds Fault with Sinners	91

15	Conclusions	93
15.1	What God Predestined	93
15.2	God's Purposes in Creation	93
15.3	How Events Are Brought to Pass	94
15.4	God's Free Choices	94
15.5	Our Free Choices	94
15.6	How Should I Feel About This?	95

Scripture Index ... 99

Preface

*I have heard of You by the hearing of the ear,
but now my eye sees You.*
—Job 42:5

We learn about God and *hear* testimonies of His greatness in the Bible. But when we consider what His hands have made, then that which He has created rises up and *shows* us something of His greatness. Truly, *"His invisible attributes are clearly seen, being understood by the things that are made, even His eternal power and Godhead"* (Rom. 1:20).

We must acknowledge our lowly and inadequate capacities to see and understand both the vastness and intricacies of what He has created. But through His creation we may glimpse a sliver of His awesomeness.

I always knew infinity is a big number. But in writing this book, I realized it is much larger than I ever imagined.

I knew God is great. But now I see He is **far** greater than it is **possible** for us to ever imagine. For the Scriptures say that He *"is able to do **far more** abundantly beyond **all** that we ... **think**"* (Eph. 3:20 NASB). No, it has never entered into the heart of man how great is our God!

Chapter 1

Introduction

*He chose us in Him before the foundation of the world, ...
having predestined us to adoption as sons by Jesus Christ to
Himself according to the good pleasure of His will.*
—Ephesians 1:4–5

*Without your consent I did not want to do anything,
so that your goodness would not be, in effect,
by compulsion but of your own free will.*
—Philemon 14 NASB

The verses above show there are at least some things God has "*predestined*," and that we have a "*will*." Discussions about predestination and our will can arouse significant emotional responses. That should not be surprising, for one's views of what God has ordained in His creation can raise questions and troubling issues such as:

- Has God purposefully created a world with evil in it?
- Can God prevent evil acts, or protect us from them?

Also, our beliefs about the extent to which God has destined[1] what happens and where we will spend eternity can greatly affect how we feel about the purpose and value of our life. For instance, people's beliefs may cause them to ask:

---

[1] In the sense of "to designate, assign, or dedicate in advance"—the second definition of "destine" from *Merriam-Webster's Dictionary and Thesaurus* (Springfield, MA: Merriam-Webster, 2007, ISBN 978-0-87779-640-4), 215.

Predestination and Our Will

- Do I have free will?
- Can my prayers influence God?
- If God has predestined who will be saved, why should I care about how I live—what difference does it make?

Although one's beliefs about these topics may raise troubling questions like those above, some people's views of what they would like the *answers* to those questions to be may have swayed their *beliefs*.

As those who believe in the God of the Bible, we would like to conform all of our beliefs, as well as the answers to any related questions (such as those above), to the truths He has written to us in His Word (2 Tim. 3:16; 1 Thess. 2:3, 13; Luke 8:21).

Because God is good, we can expect a right understanding of those truths will not be troubling nor depressing, but rather encouraging and inspiring. Indeed, looking carefully at what the Bible teaches, we will find that the way God has made things is both astonishing and wonderful!

The quotes at the top of this chapter show that not only God has a *"will,"* but we also have our *"own free will"* (as the Bible uses that phrase). Philemon 14 distinguishes doing something of our own free will from doing something *"by compulsion."* And Ephesians 1:4–5 teaches us that God has plainly *"predestined"* some things.

The Greek verb rendered *"predestined"* in Ephesians 1:5 can be used to refer to **anything** which God 'previously destined': *"**whatever** ... [He] determined before to be done"* (Acts 4:28). In fact, it is the Greek word rendered *"determined before"* in Acts 4:28. The same Greek word has been rendered *"ordained"* in 1 Corinthians 2:7. Accordingly, these three biblical terms—*predestined, determined before*, and *ordained*—are all used interchangeably herein.

The term *predestination* does not appear in the NKJV translation of the Bible, nor in the other English translations that this book occasionally quotes from—the NASB, LITV, and YLT. It will be used here to refer to **"the Bible's teaching about what God has predestined."**

Introduction

Common definitions of predestination today include a view of *what* God has predestined. But we will not begin by presupposing **any** part of the Bible's teaching about it.

Notice that none of this discussion has yet included any notion of *how* the events God has destined come to pass. For instance, it has not said things like "God *causes* us to...." However, we will certainly examine what the Scriptures teach about that, while being careful not to go beyond what they teach.[2]

This book starts with simple definitions of "*will*" that both fit the Bible's use and enable us to understand the Bible's fundamental teaching about these topics and their relationship. Subsequent chapters look at how our will is formed, and then go on to establish whether we are responsible for our willing choices and whether those choices make a difference.

The chapters which then follow examine the Bible's teaching about predestination, and how that teaching is compatible with its teaching about our will. *What* things has God predestined? *When* did He do so? *How* does what He has destined come to pass? Are we *able* to make choices contrary to what God has ordained? How can we understand the paradox between predestination and our ability to choose according to our will, as presented in the Scriptures?

We will see how the Bible shows that God does not tempt us to sin, nor does He share in the evil of our sins. And we will consider some things the Scriptures say about why God created this universe in which both good and evil are done.

We will seek the answers to all of these questions and issues from what has been written to us in the Scriptures "*for doctrine, ... for correction, for instruction in righteousness*" (2 Tim. 3:16). Quotations from the Bible are printed in red and italicized so that readers may more easily distinguish and refer to those words of truth when evaluating what is said about them.

---

[2] As we are warned in Prov. 30:6, "*Do not add to His words, lest He rebuke you, and you be found a liar.*"

Chapter 2

Our Will

*I much urged him that he come to you ...,
but it was not altogether his will that he come now.*
—1 Corinthians 16:12 LITV

We know within ourselves that we are composed of more than just our physical bodies—that we are more than just a collection of trillions of chemical reactions that occur for a period of time and then stop. We have an awareness that we are a single being with a consciousness. That is because God has formed within each of us a soul: *"God formed the man out of dust from the ground, and blew into his nostrils the breath of life; and man became a living soul"* (Gen. 2:7 LITV; see also Matt. 10:28). David rejoiced in his soul, saying, *"I will praise You, for I am fearfully and wonderfully made; marvelous are Your works, and that my soul knows very well"* (Ps. 139:14).

Unlike something *we* would be able to create, which would be strictly limited to what we could construct with inanimate, physical materials, God has made each of us with both physical and spiritual parts that, altogether, make up our person. Somehow, our body and spiritual components communicate and interact, and the body without the spirit is dead (James 2:26; Ps. 146:4; Luke 8:55; John 19:30).

Wondrously, God has created people with many mental faculties and the ability to feel and sense many things, both emotional and physical. He made us to be self-reflective (Luke 18:4–5; Ps. 119:59), to be able to reason (Isa. 1:18), and to judge (Acts 4:19). He gave us a conscience, so that by nature we have some internal testimony of what is morally good and evil (Rom. 2:14–15). We can feel pain or pleasure, compassion, love, and grief. He made us with a spiritual heart,[3] and also a will.

The things God has made in the universe around us indicate He takes pleasure in extraordinary diversity. Galaxy differs from galaxy, and star differs from star (1 Cor. 15:41). Even the planets in our solar system differ greatly from each other. Consider the tremendous diversity in the animal kingdom. It is even thought possible there will never be two, identical, large snowflakes among the approximately one septillion snowflakes that fall each year.[4]

In the same way, it has pleased God to give each of us a unique body.[5] So too, He has made our spiritual components distinctive. For instance, one person's heart has different affections from another's.

2.1 Definitions

What then is the will? There has been much philosophizing and debate about the will, both secular and religious, for thousands of years. *Will* is used in three different ways in this book, each with its own meaning. For our purposes, as an entity, the *will* can be simply defined as "a mental faculty that provides the ability to prefer or desire one thing or choice over another."[6] Others may have different or augmented definitions of what they call the *will*, but that does not matter to what is written here.

---

[3] "*He forms the heart; He understands all their works*" (Ps. 33:15 LITV), and "*The LORD ... forms the spirit of man within him*" (Zech. 12:1).

[4] Is it True that No Two Snow Crystals are Alike? (2019). *Library of Congress Everyday Mysteries*. Retrieved July 18, 2023, from https://www.loc.gov/everyday-mysteries/meteorology-climatology/item/is-it-true-that-no-two-snow-crystals-are-alike/

[5] Dr. Claire Asher described, "Even identical twins—who have the same DNA ... —have slightly different fingerprints," in Why Do Identical Twins Have Different Fingerprints? (2021). *BBC Science Focus*. Retrieved July 18, 2023, from https://www.sciencefocus.com/the-human-body/why-do-identical-twins-have-different-fingerprints-2/

[6] We may not *like* something we prefer—it may be just "least unliked."

Our Will

A different meaning for the noun *will* is found in the question, "What is your will?"—referring to "what one prefers or desires." Someone might answer, "My will is to see this happen," or, "My will is to do that."

Further, those two different answers to "What is your will?" are examples of two different ways in which one may hold a preference. The first way concerns what one would like to see occur in the sense of what one would hope for or find pleasurable. The second way concerns what one prefers given the reality of actual circumstances and various motives.

Here are definitions for the three different ways the noun *will* is used in this book:

> **will** (noun) :
> **(1)** a mental faculty that provides the ability to prefer or desire one thing or choice over another
> **(2)** what one prefers or desires:
> **(2a)** what one would hope for or find pleasurable, though not necessarily what is practical, possible, or conducive to fulfilling other purposes
> **(2b)** what one prefers given various purposes and the reality of actual circumstances

For instance, in accordance with definition (2b), it is God's *will* to bring various trials on us, if necessary, that grieve us (1 Pet. 1:6–7). But even *"though He causes grief, yet He will show compassion ... For He does not afflict **willingly** [definition (2a)]"* (Lam. 3:32–33). Similarly, we could say that it was not God's *will* (2a) for His Son to be crucified. But because of God's great love for us, it was His *will* (2b) to make Jesus a sacrifice for our sins (John 3:16; Isa. 53:10). Some who saw Jesus weeping with those who mourned Lazarus' death thought His grief showed He was not able to keep Lazarus from dying (John 11:33–37). They erred because they did not understand that Jesus has a *will* (2a) that is different from His *will* (2b).

2.2 Its Use in the Bible

The Greek noun θέλημα (Strong's #2307, transliterated here *thelema*) is the word rendered *"will"* in Ephesians 1:5 (quoted at the top of chapter 1). *Thelema* also appears in three other places in Ephesians 1. One of them is Ephesians 1:11: *"being predestined according to the purpose of Him who works all things according to the counsel of His **will**."*

Of the more than sixty times *thelema* appears in the New Testament, the NKJV translators rendered it *"will"* in all but one case. In that one case, they rendered it *"desires."* In each of the places *thelema* appears, one of the definitions of *will* previously given fits its use.

The noun *thelema* is from the Greek verb θέλω (Strong's #2309, transliterated here *thelo*). The verb *thelo* is found more than two hundred times in the New Testament. In Philippians 2:13, it is inflected as an infinitive and rendered *"to will"*: *"It is God who works in you both **to will** and to do for His good pleasure."*

We could slightly modify definition (2) previously given for the **noun** *will* ("what one prefers or desires") to create a definition for a corresponding **verb** *will*: "to prefer or desire." Happily, that definition fits well in every place *thelo* has been used in the New Testament.

> **will** (verb) : to prefer or desire

2.3 Our Willing Choices

It was not *necessary* for God to create us with a will; He could have made us without one. But, according to His good pleasure, He chose to give us one. As the previously quoted verses from Ephesians 1:5 and 11 show, God also has a will. So, one of the numerous ways God has created us in His image (Gen. 1:26–27) is by creating us with a will.

We may observe that God has also given us an ability to make choices according to our will. According to our will, we might choose whether to take, refrain from, or stop taking an action. Such actions could include directing our inner thoughts—for instance, whether to think about a necessary task at hand, a future concern, or a past experience.

It seems evident that out of all possible actions we might take at a particular moment, we choose the one that we prefer. That is, we choose the action that is according to our will in the sense of definition (2b). In this way, we could consider all of our choices to be **"willing choices."** And that is the simple, intended meaning of *willing choices* in this book: choices made according to our will (2b).

Of course, the choices available to us may be limited or constrained by circumstances (including our capabilities or resources). We may also find ourselves coerced or compelled (think "gun to your head") to prefer something that would otherwise not be our will.

God, alone, is able to work "*all things according to the counsel of His will*" (Eph. 1:11) because He is not *limited* in what He may work, nor may He be *coerced* or *compelled* to do what would otherwise not be His will. The statement that God works according to the counsel of His will means that the advisement of His will, and nothing else, determines what He chooses to work. As it is written, "*He does according to **His will** in the army of heaven and among the inhabitants of the earth. No one can **restrain** His hand*" (Dan. 4:35).

The situation that God does His will without any constraint, coercion, or compulsion, is sometimes described by saying that He does "**what He pleases**." In a similar way, a wealthy, single woman who owns a modest home might decorate it as she pleases—with her willing choices uninfluenced by considering costs or the conflicting will of another. That is the way in which Psalm 135:6 uses *pleases* when it tells us, "***Whatever** the* Lord ***pleases** He **does**, in heaven and in earth, in the seas and in all deep places.*"

Even though we choose our actions according to our will, our feelings (as also God's) in taking those actions can vary greatly. We might do them happily, grudgingly, or even angrily. We might do them joyfully or sorrowfully, rejoicing or lamenting.

In the context of that reality, 2 Corinthians 9:7 teaches us an important aspect of giving in a way that pleases God: "*So let each one give as he purposes in his heart, not **grudgingly** or of **necessity**; for God loves a cheerful giver.*" A cheerful giver is not giving with grief or because of compulsion. If thanked, one might cheerfully say with a warm smile, "I was happy to do it."

That teaching should not surprise us. Would we expect that God delights in charitable deeds done grudgingly or out of compulsion?

Chapter 3

What Influences Our Will

If the mighty works which were done in you had been done in Tyre and Sidon, they would have repented.
—Matthew 11:21–22

A number of factors that influence our will are categorized and described in the sections that follow.

3.1 Ordinary Deliberation and Persuasion

Our will concerning a particular matter may be formed or influenced by our understanding of and reasoning about our different options, together with our judgments regarding the desirability of the benefits and the dearness of the costs of each option. In a related way, our will can be affected by counsel and instruction. That is a reason the Bible's pages are **full** of teaching designed to persuade us to choose what is good and refuse what is evil. Turning to any short passage in Proverbs should provide a ready example.

Satan successfully persuaded Eve to choose to eat of the fruit of the tree of the knowledge of good and evil. And we are shown, in her deliberations in Genesis 3:6, an example of how someone's will regarding a matter may be formed.

Having an appetite, Eve saw that *"the tree was good for food."* Having an appreciation for beauty, she saw that *"it was pleasant to the eyes."* Esteeming wisdom, she saw that it was *"desirable to make one wise."* God had made Eve with an appetite for food, an appreciation for beauty, and esteeming wisdom, and those attributes were not sinful. Rather, they were "*very good*" (Gen. 1:31).

Nevertheless, there was a reason above all reasons for Eve **not** to eat of that tree's fruit: God had commanded Adam not to, for if he did, he would surely die (Gen. 2:16–17). However, Satan persuaded Eve not to believe God, but to believe that He had ulterior motives and had lied (Gen. 3:4–5).

3.2 Faith and Repentance

Adam, who also ate of the tree's forbidden fruit, showed his own wrong beliefs about God: He thought he could hide from Him in the garden (Gen. 3:8–10)![7] Similarly, Cain did not truly believe in God, for he thought he could kill his brother, hide his body in the ground, and God would not know (Gen. 4:8–10). Even more, Cain answered God insolently when He asked where his brother was!

These last examples—Eve, Adam, and Cain—show that our will is influenced by our faith and repentance (or lack thereof).

In any situation in which we have desires that are contrary to God's will, faith—a true and trusting belief in God—can make our will be to do His will. For faith causes us to understand that "*there is a way that seems right to a man, but its end is the way of death*" (Prov. 14:12; 16:25)—that we should lean not on our own understanding, but to trust in the Lord with all our heart (Prov. 3:5). Our faith also encourages us that in keeping God's commands "*there is great reward*" (Ps. 19:11).

As the New Testament uses the word *repentance*, "It is a resolve to obey God."[8] Therefore, the will of someone who is repentant can be changed by the answer to the question, "**Must** I make this particular choice in order to obey God?" If the answer is, "Yes," then it should be the repentant person's will to make that choice.

---

[7] God reproved those who have such foolish thoughts in Ps. 94:7–9, saying, "*They say, 'The LORD does not see' ... you fools ... He who formed the eye, shall He not see?*"

[8] Douglas Daudelin, *Repentance and Grace* (Allamuchy, NJ: Word Of Grace And Truth, 2022, ISBN 979-8-9867423-0-4), 24.

3.3 How We Have Been Made and Molded

We know that one person's will in a given set of circumstances may be different from another's in identical circumstances. Our will is not necessarily influenced by the circumstances alone—even if we include in them our personal circumstances, such as our health (Job 2:4–5), finances (Prov. 30:8–9), and the desires and involvement of those who are important to us (Gen. 3:12).

Our will is also shaped by the sum of the particular characteristics with which God has made each of us. For example, those characteristics that affect our will may include whether God made us male or female (*"Have you not read that He who made them at the beginning 'made them male and female'?"* Matt. 19:4), and how He made our heart (*"He fashions their hearts individually,"* Ps. 33:15) and spirit (*"The LORD ... forms the spirit of man within him,"* Zech. 12:1) and body (*"For You formed my inward parts; You wove me in my mother's womb,"* Ps. 139:13 NASB).

Our personality, character, desires, disposition (for instance, a repentant disposition), and past experiences may all influence our will. The experiences that proceed from our choices in one circumstance can influence our will in future circumstances. They may make us proud, or help to humble our hearts. They might work to give us a broken and contrite spirit.

The Bible teaches that pain and trials are experiences that can work significant changes within us that affect our will. It is written in Proverbs 20:30, *"Blows that hurt cleanse away evil, as do stripes the inner depths of the heart."*

The psalmist tells us of a transforming experience he had: *"Before I was afflicted I went astray, but now I keep Your word"* (Ps. 119:67). In the last chapter of the book of Job, he described the transformation his affliction wrought in him, saying, *"Therefore I abhor myself, and repent in dust and ashes"* (Job 42:6). Repenting involves changing your heart and spirit, as Ezekiel 18:30–31 describes, *"Repent, and turn from all your transgressions, ... and get yourselves a new heart and a new spirit."*

As an example of how people's wills may differ, and how they may be affected differently by experiences, consider what Jesus said in comparing four cities in the passage in Matthew 11:20–22. Even though Jesus had done mighty works (miracles) in Chorazin and Bethsaida, they did not repent. In rebuking those cities, and telling of the judgment they would suffer as a result, He said to them,

> *Woe to you, Chorazin! Woe to you, Bethsaida! For if the mighty works which were done in you had been done in Tyre and Sidon,* **they would have repented** *long ago in sackcloth and ashes. But I say to you, it will be more tolerable for Tyre and Sidon in the day of judgment than for you.* (vv. 21–22)

If the miraculous works Jesus did in those cities had been done long ago in Tyre and Sidon, *they* would have repented. But those miracles were not done in Tyre and Sidon, and they did not repent as a result of the testimony they *had* been given. Therefore, they too perished in their sins and will suffer in the day of judgment.

Although it was not the will of any of those four cities to repent, Jesus made known to us it *would have* been Tyre and Sidon's will to repent if they had experienced the same miracles that Chorazin and Bethsaida had. It is interesting to note that because Tyre and Sidon "*would have repented,*" Chorazin and Bethsaida will suffer more in the judgment for not having repented (as Jesus said, "**Woe to you,** *Chorazin ... [and] Bethsaida!* **For***...*").

3.4 Adam's Sin

In the beginning, everything that God "*had made ... was very good*" (Gen. 1:31). But when Adam sinned, "*sin entered the world, and death through sin, and thus death spread to all men, because all sinned*" (Rom. 5:12).

This describes that as a result of Adam's sin, all of the children he begot, and in turn the children they begot,[9] were conceived with their

---

[9] Which includes all people except Jesus, who was begotten by the Holy Spirit (Matt. 1:18, 20; Luke 1:35).

What Influences Our Will

nature corrupted. In particular, the Scriptures tell us that we are conceived in sin (Ps. 51:5) and are born *"dead in trespasses and sins"* (Eph. 2:1) and *"slaves of sin"* (Rom. 6:17)—*"fulfilling the desires of the flesh and ... by [our corrupted]* **nature** *children of wrath"* (Eph. 2:3).[10]

It seems evident that this corrupted nature operates upon one's will so as to make fulfilling the desires of one's flesh more attractive and to mute some other influences (such as the urgings of our conscience or warnings of the possible consequences of fulfilling those desires).

3.5 Being Enticed by Our Lusts

James 1:14–15 describes a means by which someone who has previously willed *not* to sin in a particular way, may have their will changed and go on to sin in that way: *"Each one is tempted when he is carried away and enticed by his own lust. Then when lust has conceived [sin*[11]*], it gives birth to sin"* (NASB).

The Greek verb rendered *"tempted"* here is πειράζω (Strong's #3985), and it has a few different meanings in its New Testament use. It can refer to an external trial (as in Rev. 2:10), or an external provocation to sin (as in Matt. 4:1). We are told that it is used in James 1:14 (*"tempted* **when**...") to refer specifically to an internal temptation in which one is enticed by his own lust. It does not explicitly describe what the *nature* of that enticing is—*what it means* to be carried away and enticed—which is *to be tempted*.

I believe it is apparent in this context that one is *"being tempted"* (James 1:13 NASB) when he is **seriously considering whether it may be his will to sin** in a particular way. This definition also

---

[10] Satan also corrupted his nature when he sinned, for the Bible describes that he was *"the seal of perfection, full of wisdom and perfect in beauty ...* **perfect** *in ... [his]* **ways** *from the day ... [he was] created, till iniquity was found in [him]"* (Ezek. 28:12, 15). But then it recounts to Satan, *"Your heart was lifted up because of your beauty; you* **corrupted** *your wisdom for the sake of your splendor"* (Ezek. 28:17). Now, *"whenever he [Satan] speaks a lie, he speaks from his own [corrupted]* **nature**" (John 8:44 NASB).

[11] For it is plain that one gives birth to what has been conceived.

matches what people often mean when they say they are being tempted—that something is causing them to consider doing something wrong or ignoble. The *means* of this enticement in James is one's "*own lust*."

Then, "lust conceives sin" when it *further* works to make it **one's will to sin** in that way. The naturally expected consequence of having conceived sin—giving birth to sin—occurs when the one who now wills to sin naturally **takes actions to sin** in that way.

Of course, this process could be interrupted at any point along the way. But if, after giving birth to this sin, the will to commit it continues, then one goes on to *practice* it, and it becomes *full-grown*. The one who committed adultery becomes an adulterer, the one who tried drugs becomes an addict. That is the fourth stage described in this passage in James: "*And sin, when it is full-grown, brings forth death*" (James 1:15).

The language used in this description is interesting: One is enticed by his lust (which is a feminine noun in the Greek), his lust conceives sin, and then gives birth to it. It brings to mind the woman with a harlot's dress in Proverbs 7:6–27, who went out seeking a man to commit adultery. "*With her enticing speech she caused him to yield, with her flattering lips she seduced him. Immediately he went after her, as an ox goes to the slaughter*" (vv. 21–22).

3.6 Spirits

Our will can be influenced not only by our own spirit, but by other spirits, whether it be:

- the **Holy Spirit**: "*[Saul sought to kill David.] So he went there to Naioth in Ramah. Then the Spirit of God was upon him also, and [instead of continuing to seek to kill David] he went on and prophesied ... And he also stripped off his clothes ... and [King Saul] lay down naked all that day and all that night*" (1 Sam. 19:23–24), or
- **Satan**: "*Now Satan stood up against Israel, and moved David to number Israel*" (1 Chron. 21:1); "*Ananias, why has Satan filled your heart to lie to the Holy Spirit?*" (Acts 5:3)

or
- **demons**: *"There met ... [Jesus] a man with an unclean spirit ... And always, night and day, he was in the mountains and in the tombs, crying out and cutting himself with stones. ... [After Jesus cast out the demons, the people in the city] came to Jesus, and saw the one who had been demon-possessed and had the legion, sitting and clothed and in his right mind"* (Mark 5:2, 5, 15); when an unclean spirit leaves a man, that man's ordinary will to keep his *"house [himself] ... swept, and put in order"* is restored (Matt. 12:43–44).[12]

3.7 God Turning a Heart

God has not only fashioned people's hearts individually (Ps. 33:15), but He can subsequently influence a heart's desires. Psalm 105:25 states that God *"turned"* the heart of the Egyptians *"to hate His people."* The Scriptures tell us that *"The king's heart is in the hand of the* LORD, *like the rivers of water; He **turns** it wherever He wishes"* (Prov. 21:1). Although the Lord can *directly* influence our will (as section 3.11 will address), the accounts in the Bible usually describe Him turning the king's heart through events and persuasion, as well as through other influences described in this chapter.

One account in which we are told *how* God turned a king's heart is when He desired to kill Ahab according to the judgment He had pronounced against him in 1 Kings 21:19. Ahab was one of the most wicked kings of Israel who ever lived (1 Kings 21:25), and God had determined to bring judgment upon him by killing him in battle at Ramoth Gilead (1 Kings 22:20).

In that context, we are told that *"the king of Israel and Jehoshaphat the king of Judah ... **sat each on his throne**"* (1 Kings 22:10) to

---

[12] However, I do not believe that a demon is able to dwell in those who are *"a temple of God"* and in whom *"the Spirit of God dwells"* (1 Cor. 3:16 NASB; see also Rom. 8:9–11). The *Holy* Spirit and an *unclean* spirit cannot dwell together in the same "house" (*"He who works deceit shall not dwell within my house,"* Ps. 101:7). In Jesus' description of an unclean spirit who once leaves but then returns to dwell in a man again, He made explicit that He was describing a case in which the spirit finds his former house now *"empty"* (Matt. 12:43–45).

decide whether to go up to fight against Ramoth Gilead. And about four hundred of Ahab's prophets unanimously told him to go up, for the Lord would deliver it into his hand (1 Kings 22:6, 12).

But at Jehoshaphat's request, they brought the only (true) prophet of the Lord who was left in Israel, Micaiah (1 Kings 22:7–9), and he prophesied *"the word of the LORD"* (v. 19). Micaiah said that he had seen *"the LORD **sitting on His throne**, and all the host of heaven standing by, on His right hand and on His left"* (v. 19). Though to earthly eyes it appeared that the two kings on their earthly thrones would rule over whether to send their armies to war, Micaiah told of One seated on His throne far above them.[13] And in fact, He would turn the hearts of those kings to accomplish His good purposes—as we read in Proverbs 21:1.

The assembly in heaven which Micaiah described appears to be an assembly like that described in Job 1:6, where both good and evil spirits alike—*"**all** the host of heaven ... on His **right** ... and on His left"*—were gathered before God. In that earlier assembly described in Job 1, Satan expressed his desire to see all that Job had been blessed with taken from him and to see Job curse God as a result (vv. 10–11). For such is Satan's delight. And God chose to permit Satan to work out the evil in his heart—to do whatever he willed with all that Job had. Nevertheless, as one could have been assured from Romans 8:28 (*"we know that all things work together for good to those who love God"*), the evil which God permitted Satan to do did not result in Job's destruction, but in his sanctification and blessing (Job 42:5–6, 12–15).

Micaiah prophesied that in this heavenly assembly, God asked, *"Who will persuade Ahab to go up, that he may fall at Ramoth Gilead?"* (1 Kings 22:20) Of course, God did not ask this question so that He might find out. He asked it in the way He asked Adam, *"Where are you?"* (Gen. 3:9) or Cain, *"Where is Abel your brother?"* (Gen. 4:9) or the disciples on the road to Emmaus, *"What things?"* (Luke 24:19) or Satan, *"From where have you come? And ... [why]* have you set

---

[13] *"For You, LORD, are most high above all the earth; You are exalted far above all gods"* (Ps. 97:9).

What Influences Our Will

your heart on My servant Job?" (Job 1:7–8 LITV)[14]

By His question, He made known to the assembly 1) that Ahab would die if he went up to battle, 2) that he would not go up unless he was persuaded, and 3) that God would permit someone to attempt to persuade him.

Eventually, a spirit who desired to see Ahab die said that he would persuade Ahab by being a lying spirit in the mouth of all of Ahab's prophets. By doing so, that spirit displayed two predominant characteristics of the devil and those of whom he is the father. Jesus described those characteristics in John 8:44: The devil *"was a murderer from the beginning"* and *"a liar and the father of it."* God responded by 1) making known that Ahab would be persuaded by the lying spirit, and 2) permitting that spirit to go out and do according to his will (1 Kings 22:22).

God then **told** these things to Ahab through His prophet Micaiah—who spoke the truth in the name of the Lord, making known to him the situation that was occurring in front of them. Nevertheless, Ahab was persuaded by the lying spirit that spoke through his four hundred prophets—even as God had said he would be (1 Kings 22:23–29)!

3.8 God Giving Restraint

We are shown in Romans 1:28–29 that God is able to give people over to a depraved mind: *"God gave them over to a depraved mind, to do those things which are not proper, being filled with all unrighteousness"* (NASB). To give people **over to** a depraved mind is different from **giving** them a depraved mind. It presupposes they **have** a depraved mind, and that God can give them a level of **restraint** in what they do.

God can enable someone with a depraved mind to have some restraint when it comes to their will to give in to and work out the unrighteous desires of that mind. That restraint someone may exercise is often called *self-control*. Because of God's ability to

---

[14] Ezekiel, not knowing the answer to a question he was asked, well replied, *"Lord GOD, You know"* (Ezek. 37:3).

restrain us from sin, the psalmist pleads with God, *"Establish my footsteps in Your word, and do not let any iniquity have dominion over me"* (Ps. 119:133 NASB).

3.9 Hardening One's Own Heart
As we read earlier in Proverbs 20:30, painful trials can naturally cleanse the inner depths of the heart from evil. A heart that is changed by such a trial is like a wrestler who is in a painful hold that is getting more painful every moment, and "taps out" before suffering a serious injury (or suffering a further injury).

A hardened heart is one that resists such changes, and persists undaunted in its desires in spite of hard and painful consequences. It is like a wrestler who is particularly stoic or motivated, who "steels himself" to endure much suffering without tapping out. Pharaoh hardened his heart (Ex. 8:15, 32; 9:34) so that he would not let the Israelites go, despite a number of miraculous, destructive plagues that were brought on Egypt.

3.10 God Hardening One's Heart
God can also harden someone's heart. And He is able to make a heart so hard, so unwilling to bend or give, to soften and yield, that it obstinately resists *any* external pressures to "tap out"—**persisting** in its affections and desires in a way no heart would ever naturally do. For instance, He hardened Pharaoh's heart so that he refused to let the Israelites go until the end of ten miraculous plagues (Ex. 11:10)—which destroyed Egypt (Ex. 10:7) and killed all of their firstborn (Num. 33:4). And even after Pharaoh *had* let the Israelites go, God hardened the Egyptians' hearts such that they pursued them even down into the parted Red Sea (Ex. 14:17), to their own deaths, instead of being halted in the fear of God, finally realizing they *must* let them go.

If God were to harden a heart intent on going after its sinful desires so hard that there is no *possibility* for that heart to turn from those sins, then there would be no possibility for repentance and forgiveness. In such a case, that heart would be like the heart of fallen angels—for whom there is no Savior nor provision to be forgiven (Heb. 2:16), and therefore no purpose for repenting nor ability to repent.

We know that God's longsuffering toward unrepentant sinners, though great, has limits,[15] and that limit has certainly been reached when they die. After they have died, the possibility of salvation no longer remains for them (Luke 16:26; 2 Cor. 5:10), but only the fearful day of judgment and eternal punishment with "*the devil and his angels*" in the lake of fire (Matt. 25:41, 46; Rev. 20:10, 15).

Since the Bible never speaks of those who have died in their sins subsequently coming to repentance (but instead, for instance, gnashing their teeth), and salvation is no longer possible for them, I expect that in that state God has hardened their hearts permanently. As they desired such an impenitent heart while they lived, so they will have it forever.

3.11 God's Direct Influence

The Scriptures show that God can also directly influence a person's will. For instance, "*The Lord opened her [Lydia's] heart to heed the things spoken by Paul*" (Acts 16:14). Another example is found in Ezra 1:1: "*That the word of the LORD by the mouth of Jeremiah might be fulfilled, the LORD stirred up the spirit of Cyrus king of Persia, so that he made a proclamation throughout all his kingdom.*" Regarding believers, we are told in Philippians 2:13, "*God ... **works in you** both **to will** and to do for His good pleasure.*"

Note that all of the above are *good* influences. God may give us a desire, or incline our hearts, to do what is good—as He opened Lydia's heart to heed the things Paul was speaking, and as He works in all believers "*to will ... for His good pleasure.*" So also, He worked good in the wills of both Saul and the messengers Saul sent when he was seeking to kill David: The Spirit of God came upon them and made them will to prophesy with the prophets instead of

---

[15] As it is written in Rom. 2:4–5: "*Or do you despise the riches of His goodness, forbearance, and longsuffering, not knowing that the goodness of God leads you to repentance? But in accordance with your hardness and your impenitent heart you are treasuring up for yourself wrath in the day of wrath and revelation of the righteous judgment of God.*"

continue on to seize David (1 Sam. 19:19–24).

I am not aware of anywhere the Bible describes God directly inclining someone's will to sin or do evil. For example, section 3.5, "Being Enticed by Our Lusts," showed that when someone is carried away and enticed to sin, that enticement is "*by his own lust*" (James 1:14 NASB). James 1:13 explicitly tells us that temptation is not "*by God*," for He "*does not tempt anyone*" (NASB). More will be said about this in section 14.4, "God Does Not Tempt Us to Sin."

In section 3.8, "God Giving Restraint," we saw that God giving people *over to* a depraved mind is actually the tempering of a good thing—restraint or "self-control"—that He might otherwise graciously give. That is very different from *giving* someone a depraved mind. Similarly, in section 3.10, "God Hardening One's Heart," we saw that God's hardening of a heart merely keeps it from changing its present affections—from softening, yielding, or repenting. In doing so, He does not put within that heart new, sinful affections.

3.12 God Giving a New Heart

In addition to all of the previously described influences on our will, God can give someone a new heart: "*I will give you a new heart and put a new spirit within you; I will take the heart of stone out of your flesh and give you a heart of flesh*" (Ezek. 36:26). He does that when He saves people, putting His Holy Spirit in them to dwell in them (Rom. 8:9, 11; John 7:38–39), making them new creations (2 Cor. 5:17; Gal. 6:15; John 3:3; Matt. 9:17), cleansing their hearts by the sprinkling of Jesus' blood (Heb. 9:14; 10:22; 12:24), and putting His "*laws into their hearts, and in their minds*" (Heb. 10:16; also Heb. 8:10 and Jer. 31:33). This was made possible by Jesus' dying on the cross for our sins, so that "*as by one man's disobedience [Adam's sin] many were made sinners, so also by one Man's obedience many will be made righteous*" (Rom. 5:19).

Chapter 4

Can We Choose Our Will?

[This] is to ask whether a man can will what he wills.
—John Locke[16]

Apart from the ways our will may be influenced, we might ask if we can choose our will. The question that is intended here, and its answer, may be better understood by considering a question that has similar issues: Can we choose what we believe?

It is plain that we cannot choose whether we *believe* something—we either believe it or not. We *can* seek to determine whether something is true, to learn about it and have a heart to receive the truth (even in the face of apparent grave consequences). And that seeking may help us come to believe it, or result in our believing—for Jesus said, "*Seek, and you will find*" (Luke 11:9; see also Rom. 10:14).

In the same way, we cannot choose *our will* regarding a particular matter—our will is what it is. As described in chapter 3, our will can be *influenced* and changed by many things, including our deliberations and consideration of various criteria that we think significant. It may also be affected by our seeking wisdom and counsel about a matter (when there is a willingness to receive it). However, in the end, although we can choose **according to** our preference, we cannot

---

[16] John Locke, *An Essay Concerning Humane Understanding* (London: Eliz. Holt, 1690), book II, chapter XXI section 25. Reprinted as a Project Gutenberg ebook #10615 (2004). Retrieved August 19, 2023, from https://www.gutenberg.org/files/10615/10615-h/10615-h.htm

choose **what** our preference is. Though we can choose according to our will, we cannot choose our will.

It appears it must be the same with God's will—that it is what it is. For instance, it seems clear He has not *chosen* to hate evil. It is, as it has always been, His *nature* to hate evil. By nature, He "*is good*" (Mark 10:18). So, it appears that God is not able to choose His will—even as He "*said to Moses, 'I AM WHO I AM'*" (Ex. 3:14).

Notwithstanding, if there were unrighteousness with God (which, of course, there certainly is not), I suspect those who object to God holding us responsible for our sins would have no such qualms about accusing (rather than excusing) God. It is an exceeding blessing for us that God's will is both fully informed and surpassingly excellent in every matter!

John Locke has eloquently explained how it is self-evident that we could never be free to choose our will (and I do not know of anything the Bible says that would show we are or require us to be):

> To ask whether a man be at liberty to will ... [that] which he pleases, is to ask whether a man can will what he wills ... A question which, I think, needs no answer: and they who can make a question of it must suppose one will to determine the acts of another, and another to determine that, and so on in infinitum.[17]

Nevertheless, the understood reality for those who believe what the Scriptures teach is that we are still responsible for our willful sins (as will be shown in chapter 5), God does not share in the evil of those sins (as will be explained in section 14.3), and He justly holds us accountable for them (as will be seen in section 14.5).

---

[17] Ibid.

Chapter 5

We Are Responsible for Our Willing Choices

Walk in the ways of your heart, ... but know that for all these God will bring you into judgment.
—Ecclesiastes 11:9

God has made us such that we have an ability to make choices according to our will. The Bible shows that He has done so in such a way that we are morally responsible for those choices—even though our will can be influenced in many ways by many things. "*Responsible*" is used here to mean simply that one is rightly held accountable for something—justly receiving praise or reproof, reward or punishment for it.

Even though it was Satan who persuaded Eve that God had lied to keep her from being all that she could be, she was responsible for believing him and choosing to eat the forbidden fruit (Gen. 3:13, 16). Even though it was Satan who filled Ananias' heart to lie to the Holy Spirit so that he would appear more piously charitable to men (Acts 5:3–4), he was responsible for willfully choosing to lie (Acts 5:4–5). Even if our actions in a situation are predictable, being influenced by "*the ways of your heart*," our character and desires, we are still responsible for choosing to take them (Eccles. 11:9)—whether for praise or blame.

I expect this state of affairs makes sense to most people. Even though Judas was driven by his love of money to steal (John 12:6) and betray the Messiah unto death (Matt. 26:14–16), I expect most are not surprised to see that Judas is responsible for those crimes (Luke

22:21–22; Deut. 5:19). I do not think many would accept as a defense of Judas, "Don't blame him, he just loves money!" Although there are some who would accept such a defense, those who are persuaded by God's Word should not. Judas himself came to acknowledge and confess, "*I have sinned by betraying innocent blood*" (Matt. 27:4).

Isaiah 66:3–4 is one of many places God describes how *our* willing choices affect *His* choices for us and judgments of us:

> *As **they have chosen** their own ways, and their soul **delights** in their abominations, so **I will choose** their punishments and will bring on them what they dread. **Because** ... I spoke, but they did not listen. And they did evil in My sight and chose that in which I did **not delight**.* (NASB)

We naturally feel that someone who does something noble or heroic should be commended or even rewarded, while another should be reproved or even punished for willfully doing something shameful or heinous. Romans 2:14–15 gives us a description of those natural feelings: "*Gentiles, who do not have the law, **by nature** do the things in the law, ... who show the work of the law written in their hearts, their conscience also bearing witness, and between themselves their thoughts **accusing** or else **excusing**.*"

The Scriptures confirm, in many places and ways, those natural feelings that we are able to make choices according to our will, and also that we bear moral responsibility for those choices. We are told in Ecclesiastes, "*Walk in the ways of your heart, ... but know that for all these God will bring you into judgment*" (Eccles. 11:9).

It is hard to find a chapter in the Bible that does *not* contain an example or instruction that encourages or teaches us to turn from evil or to choose what is good *because of* the various consequences we can expect as a result of those choices. Further, the Bible says that when we do what is good, God is pleased and rejoices, and when we do what is evil, He is grieved and angry. Here are a few of many examples:

My son, if your heart is wise, my heart will rejoice— ***indeed****,* ***I myself****;* ***yes****, my inmost being will rejoice* ***when*** *your lips speak right things.* (Prov. 23:15–16)

And the L*ORD* *said to Moses, "Go, get down! For your people whom you brought out of the land of Egypt have corrupted themselves. They have turned aside quickly out of the way which I commanded them. ... Now therefore, let Me alone, that My wrath may burn hot against them and I may consume them."* (Ex. 32:7–8, 10)

Therefore I have poured out My indignation on them; I have consumed them with the fire of My wrath; and I have recompensed their deeds on their own heads. (Ezek. 22:31)

Then Noah built an altar to the L*ORD**, and took of every clean animal and of every clean bird, and offered burnt offerings on the altar. And the* L*ORD* *smelled a soothing aroma.* ***Then*** *the* L*ORD* *said in His heart, "I will never again curse the ground for man's sake."* (Gen. 8:20–21)

For Your eyes are open to all the ways of the sons of men, to give everyone according to his ways and according to the fruit of his doings. (Jer. 32:19)

[God] will render ... indignation and wrath, tribulation and anguish, on every soul of man who does evil, ... but glory, honor, and peace to everyone who works what is good ... for there is no partiality with God. (Rom. 2:6, 8–11)

Chapter 6

Our Choices Make a Difference

*Your eyes are open to all the ways of the sons of men,
to give everyone according to his ways and
according to the fruit of his doings.*
—Jeremiah 32:19

We naturally feel quite strongly, and our experience agrees, that our choices usually make a difference to what happens, and those perceived differences normally make sense to us. Indeed, the different results we expect from different choices often influence our deliberations regarding the choice we prefer.

The Bible confirms those natural feelings are correct. As described earlier, almost every page of the Bible contains encouragement or teaching that we should turn from evil or choose what is good because of the various consequences we can expect those choices to bring.

An example of such teaching includes an account in 2 Chronicles 12 in which God sent the king of Egypt, Shishak, against Judah and Jerusalem because of their transgressions. God told the king of Judah through the prophet Shemaiah why He was bringing this judgment on them. But when the leaders and the king of Judah heard, they *"humbled themselves; and they said, 'The L*ORD* is righteous'"* (2 Chron. 12:6). The next verse tells us that *"**when** the L*ORD* saw that they humbled themselves,"* He said that He would not destroy them but give them some deliverance (though He made them Shishak's servants).

Another time, we are told that God helped Israel in battle against the Hagrites because they trusted in Him and cried out to Him: *"They made war with the Hagrites, ... And they were helped against them, and the Hagrites were delivered into their hand, and all who were with them,* **for** *they cried out to God in the battle. He heeded their prayer,* **because** *they put their trust in Him"* (1 Chron. 5:19–20).

Even though we know it was certain that Jesus would be delivered from every evil, Jesus needed to pray to His Father to deliver Him. Therefore, He prayed with vehement cries and tears. And we are told that *because of* that earnest pleading, His Father heard Him and answered His prayers: *"Who, in the days of His flesh,* **when** *He had offered up prayers and supplications, with vehement cries and tears to Him who was able to save Him from death, ... [He] was heard* **because of** *His godly fear"* (Heb. 5:7).

James 5:16 plainly states this fact, *"The effective, fervent prayer of a righteous man* **avails much**.*"* Conversely, James 4:2 explains to some, *"You do not have* **because** *you do not ask."*

Consider what Hezekiah did, who was gravely ill when God sent the prophet Isaiah to tell him, *"Thus says the LORD: 'Set your house in order, for you shall die, and not live'"* (2 Kings 20:1). After Isaiah left, Hezekiah cried out to the Lord for mercy, weeping bitterly and pleading with Him to remember how he had walked before Him uprightly. Then, as Isaiah was returning from delivering the message, God told him to go back and *"tell Hezekiah the leader of My people, 'Thus says the LORD, the God of David your father: "I have heard your prayer, I have seen your tears; surely I will heal you"'"* (2 Kings 20:5).

The high priest Eli provides an example of what we should not do (which is nothing). When God told Eli of the judgment He would bring on his house because of his sons' iniquity (that he was aware of but did not restrain), he did not repent, but piously said, *"It is the LORD. Let Him do what seems good to Him"* (1 Sam. 3:18). And God surely did bring that judgment.[18]

Ezra 8:22–23 makes a general statement regarding how our choices make a difference, and gives a particular example in which God responded to prayer: "*'The hand of our God is upon all those for good who seek Him, but His power and His wrath are against all those who forsake Him.'* **So** *we fasted and entreated our God for this, and He* **answered** *our prayer.*"

It is written, "*You who hear prayer, to You all flesh will come*" (Ps. 65:2), "*for He has not despised nor abhorred the affliction of the afflicted; nor has He hidden His face from him; but* **when** *he cried to Him for help, He heard*" (Ps. 22:24 NASB).

There are other general statements about the differences our choices make, such as "*Draw near to God and He will draw near to you,*" and, "*Humble yourselves in the sight of the Lord, and He will lift you up*" (James 4:8, 10). Of course, the choices of the wicked also make a difference, for their good or bad, and Ahab provides a ready example of each.

We previously read about some of God's dealings with Ahab, who was one of the most wicked kings of Israel who ever lived (1 Kings 21:25). Because of his wickedness, God sent the prophet Elijah to pronounce judgment on his house (his descendants and his wife; 1 Kings 21:21–24). However, "*when Ahab heard those words, ... he tore his clothes and put sackcloth on his body, and fasted and lay in sackcloth, and went about mourning*" (1 Kings 21:27). Because he did so, God said He would delay bringing that judgment until after Ahab was dead: "*See how Ahab has humbled himself before Me?*

---

[18] By contrast, the pagan king of Nineveh repented when God told him He would overthrow Nineveh. The king did so because, he said, "*Who can tell if God will ... turn away from His fierce anger, so that we may not perish?*" (Jonah 3:9) And because they repented, God **did** turn from destroying Nineveh (Jonah 3:10). For God has said, "*The instant I speak concerning a nation and concerning a kingdom, to pluck up, to pull down, and to destroy it, if that nation against whom I have spoken turns from its evil, I will relent of the disaster that I thought to bring upon it*" (Jer. 18:7–8).

Because *he has humbled himself before Me, I will **not** bring the calamity in his days"* (v. 29).

The Scriptures also teach us something that might not be obvious to us naturally—that even the thoughts of our heart make a difference to what happens. They tell us, *"For the eyes of the* Lord *run to and fro throughout the whole earth, to show Himself strong on behalf of those whose **heart** is loyal to Him"* (2 Chron. 16:9), and, *"For the* Lord *searches all hearts and understands all the intent of the **thoughts**. If you seek Him, He will be found by you; but if you forsake Him, He will cast you off forever"* (1 Chron. 28:9).

All that we think and choose and do affects God's dealings with us— *"For Your eyes are open to all the ways of the sons of men, to give everyone according to his ways and according to the fruit of his doings"* (Jer. 32:19). Besides the effects on God's dealings with us, it is helpful to know that our thoughts and actions *please* or *displease* Him. Would we not like God's displeasure? Then, let us make it our aim *"to be well pleasing to Him"* (2 Cor. 5:9)!

Chapter 7

We Choose, but God Determines What Happens

A man's heart plans his way, but the LORD *directs his steps.*
—Proverbs 16:9

As the phrase "***both*** *to will and to do*" (Phil. 2:13) demonstrates, **to will** is different from **doing**. We may willfully choose and plan to do something, but then find events occur that we did not expect which change our plans or that we are powerless to overcome.

James 4:13–16 warns against the "*arrogance*" of thinking we will be able to carry out our plans apart from God's will. That passage refers to God's will (definition (2b) on page 17) to permit and enable us to carry out our plans, whether those plans are good or unrighteous, without implying that He delights in or takes pleasure in them:[19]

> *Come now, you who say, "Today or tomorrow we will go to such and such a city, spend a year there, buy and sell, and make a profit"; whereas you do not know what will happen tomorrow. For what is your life? It is even a vapor that appears for a little time and then vanishes away. Instead you ought to say, "If the* **Lord wills***, we shall* **live** *and* **do** *this or that." But now you boast in your* ***arrogance****. All such boasting is evil.*

---

[19] Observe that for God to give someone time to repent requires that He permit that person to continue for a time unrepentantly pursuing what is sinful.

Lamentations 3:37 rhetorically asks, "*Who is he who speaks [saying, 'I will do this' or 'This will occur'] and it comes to pass, when the Lord has not commanded it?*" The understood answer is that the Lord has commanded all that comes to pass.

We can see this reality demonstrated in the accounts of Jesus' crucifixion. "*The chief priests, the scribes, and the elders of the people assembled ... and plotted to take Jesus by trickery and kill Him*" (Matt. 26:3–4). They plotted the most unrighteous, evil act in all of human history, and planned not to do it "*during the [Passover] feast, lest there be an uproar among the people*" (Matt. 26:5).

Yet, because God determines all that occurs in His creation, the **result** of their evil **plans** would simply be "*to **do** whatever Your hand and Your purpose **determined before** to be done*" (Acts 4:28). And God's good purpose, because of His love for the world, was to make Jesus a sacrifice for our sins, in order "*that whoever believes in Him should not perish but have everlasting life*" (John 3:16, 14–15).

Similarly, Joseph commented on the evil his brothers did by selling him into slavery: "***You** meant evil against me; but **God** meant it for good, in order to ... save many people*" (Gen. 50:20). Psalm 105:17 affirms that it was God who "***sent** a man before them—Joseph—who was sold as a slave.*"

Observe that it was **not** evil for **God** to have Joseph serve Him and His good purposes as a slave in Egypt for a time. Although Joseph could have a complaint against those who unrighteously made him a slave, he could not so complain against God for this trial He made him suffer. More will be said about that in chapter 14.

Since it was necessary for "*Christ, our Passover, ... [to be] sacrificed for us*" on the Passover (1 Cor. 5:7), the collective will of the assembled Jewish leaders to wait until *after* the Passover feast to kill Jesus needed to change. In this case, when Judas came to them offering to betray Jesus, their excitement would not permit them to wait: "*And hearing, they rejoiced and promised to give him silver*" (Mark 14:11 LITV). We can also see their lust to crucify Jesus in delaying their Passover meal to do so—eating it after morning had

We Choose, but God Determines What Happens

come, and thereby breaking the Law (as shown by John 18:[27–]28, Deut. 16:4, Ex. 34:25, and 12:10).

When Pilate was questioning Jesus, he asked, "*Do You not know that I have power to crucify You, and power to release You?*" (John 19:10) Jesus' answer implied that Pilate did indeed have power to take either action, but only because God had given him that power: "*You could have no power at all against Me unless it had been given you from above*" (v. 11). John the Baptist showed that Jesus' statement applies to **any** power or thing **anyone** may have. He told us, "*A man can receive **nothing** unless it has been given to him from heaven*" (John 3:27).

And it was not Pilate's will to crucify Jesus. After examining Him, he pronounced Him to be innocent several times, saying, "*I find no fault in Him at all*" (John 18:38; see also John 19:4, 6, and Luke 23:22). He was also afraid of Jesus (John 19:8), and warned by his wife to "*have nothing to do with that righteous Man*" (Matt. 27:19 NASB). Therefore, he "*sought to release Him*" (John 19:12).

Then why did Pilate *not* release Him? Over the course of events that morning, his will was changed. The turning point came, ironically, when the Jews threatened to accuse Pilate of not being Caesar's friend (John 19:12–13).

At the end of this chapter, we will look at an account in Isaiah 10 that tells about a king who was unwittingly carrying out God's judgment on Judah by going to war against them. As a result, God would give him success. But afterward, God would severely punish that king for crediting his victory to his own strength and wisdom. That account underscores how important it is for us to understand and believe the instruction and warning in James 4:13–16: Though we make plans in our heart, we can **do** nothing apart from the Lord's will. As Job said, "*Behold, ... He shuts against a man, and no one opens*" (Job 12:14 LITV).

The Bible teaches that God determines **all** that we do and **all** that takes place in His creation in many passages, and without contradiction. Here are sixteen short passages which describe that.

Note that some verses in the first two paragraphs make an interesting distinction between 1) the plans we make in our heart according to our will, and 2) our actions. They appear to indicate that we have peculiar ownership of our heart's thoughts and plans.[20]

> "*A **man's heart plans** his way, but **the LORD directs** his steps*" (Prov. 16:9). God kept Abimelech from adultery because it was with an upright heart he had taken Sarah, and told him, "*Yes, I know that you did this in the integrity of your heart. ... **therefore** I did not let you touch her*" (Gen. 20:6). It is as Jeremiah confessed in his prayer, "*LORD ... it is not in man who walks to direct his own steps*" (Jer. 10:23). And Proverbs 20:24 affirms, "*A man's steps are of the LORD; how then can a man understand his own way?*"

> "*The preparations of the heart **belong to man**, but the answer of the tongue is **from the LORD**"* (Prov. 16:1). This verse shows that God's determination of our actions in His creation extends also to the words we speak in it!

Even the outcome of casting a lot is determined by God: "*The lot is cast into the lap, but its every decision is from the LORD*" (Prov. 16:33). King Ahab demonstrated this in his death. When he went up to battle at Ramoth Gilead, he disguised himself to keep from being recognized and becoming a target. But he was killed by an arrow from a man who "*drew a bow at random*" (1 Kings 22:34). Perhaps the archer thought, "I'll just shoot into this crowd and I'm sure to hit somebody." Not only did his arrow hit the king, but it "happened" to strike Ahab "*between the joints of his armor*" (1 Kings 22:34)—for Ahab's armor

---

[20] We are described as morally responsible for the thoughts of our hearts, and those thoughts are said to be a reason that God brought the judgment of the great flood in Gen. 6:5, 7: "*The LORD **saw** that the wickedness **of man** was great in the earth, and that every intent of the thoughts of **his heart** was only evil continually. ... So the LORD said, 'I will destroy man'.*" The Lord also commended David that it was in his heart to build a house for the Lord (even though He would not permit David to build it) in 2 Chron. 6:8: "***You did well** in that it **was in your heart**.*"

was not seamless.

Psalm 135:6 proclaims that *"whatever the* L*ORD* ***pleases** He **does**, in heaven and in earth, in the seas and in all deep places."* Even when events transpired which prompted unbelievers to gloat in Psalm 115:2, *"So where is their God?"* the next verse answers and affirms, *"He does **whatever He pleases**."* Similarly, Ephesians 1:11 describes God as He *"who works **all things** according to the counsel of **His will**."*

And God personally affirms the same: *"For I am God, and there is no other; I am God, ... saying, 'My counsel shall stand, and I will do **all** My **pleasure**'"* (Isa. 46:9–10). Accordingly, *"not one ... [sparrow] falls to the ground apart from your Father's will"* (Matt. 10:29).

Then, it follows that, *"if there is calamity in a city, will not the* L*ORD* *have done it?"* (Amos 3:6) God leaves no question that is indeed the case, declaring, *"I make peace and create calamity; I,* **the** L*ORD,* *do* **all** *these things"* (Isa. 45:7).

God tells us, *"Now see that **I, even I, am He, and there is no God besides Me**; I kill and I make alive; I wound and I heal; nor is there any who can deliver from My hand"* (Deut. 32:39). For *"the* L*ORD* *of hosts has sworn, saying, 'Surely, as I have thought, so it shall come to pass, and as I have purposed, so it shall stand' ... For the* L*ORD* *of hosts has purposed, and who will annul it? His hand is stretched out, and who will turn it back?"* (Isa. 14:24, 27)

But if, contrary to what the Scriptures state above, God does *not* determine all that takes place, then how could He work *"**all things** ... together for good to those who love God, to those who are the called according to His purpose"* (Rom. 8:28)? That verse could express no more than a good *intention* on God's part, and the *actuality* would be that God will try the best He can in the face of evil agents and forces in this world whose actions are not fully subject to His will.

God's determination of all that takes place in His creation also explains how He can know and prophesy to us of the future, and never be wrong: *"I am God, and there is none like Me, declaring the end from the beginning, and from ancient times things that are not yet done"* (Isa. 46:9–10).

The account in Isaiah 10 that was mentioned earlier describes the Lord's plan to send the king of Assyria against His people in Judah and Jerusalem to punish them because of their sinful ways. Because of that plan, He called the king of Assyria *"the rod of My anger and the staff in whose hand is My indignation"* (v. 5). But it tells us that the king had his own, different motives for going against Jerusalem in verses 7–11. For instance, it says, *"Yet he [the king of Assyria] does **not** mean so, nor does his heart think so; but it **is** in his heart to destroy, and cut off not a few nations"* (v. 7).

It also describes the king of Assyria's arrogant heart, *"For he says: 'By the strength of my hand I have done it, and by my wisdom, for I am prudent; ... I have put down the inhabitants like a valiant man'"* (v. 13). In response, God rebuked the king of Assyria for his proud thoughts, saying, *"Shall the ax [the king] boast itself against him who chops with it [God]? ... As if a rod could wield itself against those who lift it up!"* (v. 15)

Because of the king of Assyria's arrogance, God declared what He would do to the king once He had finished bringing His judgment on Jerusalem through him: *"Therefore it shall come to pass, when the Lord has performed all His work on Mount Zion and on Jerusalem, that He will say, 'I will punish the fruit of the **arrogant heart** of the king of Assyria, and the glory of his haughty looks'"* (v. 12).

Let us be careful then not to have such arrogant thoughts. Though we may plan and choose, we can only *"live and do"* *"if the Lord wills"* (James 4:15). He determines all that takes place in His creation, including the words that are spoken in it (Prov. 16:1). *When* He determines what takes place, and *how* those events are brought to pass, are described in chapter 8, "When Does or Did God Ordain Events?" and chapter 10, "How Ordained Events Come to Pass."

Chapter 8

When Does or Did God Ordain Events?

*He indeed was foreordained
before the foundation of the world.*
—1 Peter 1:20

We have seen that God determines all that occurs in His creation. Of course, that determination must *precede* those events, or it would simply be *observation*. David, in the Spirit, said, *"In Your book they all were written, the days fashioned for me, when as yet there were none of them"* (Ps. 139:16). This verse plainly tells us that *all* of David's days were written in God's book before even *one* of those days came to pass. That is, they were written before David existed. We might ask then, how long before David existed?

Similarly, God told Jeremiah, *"Before I formed you in the womb I knew you; before you were born ... I ordained you a prophet to the nations"* (Jer. 1:5). Before God created Jeremiah, He knew when and how He would create and form him, and for what purposes. Matthew 1:17 appears to demonstrate that the days between Abraham and the Christ (forty-two generations divided into three periods of fourteen generations) were all determined before any of those days occurred.

It is clear that God ordained *some* things that He would bring to pass in His creation before He created anything—that is, before the foundation of the world. For example, He determined that Jesus would be crucified for our sins: *"You were ... redeemed with ... the precious blood of Christ, as of a lamb without blemish and without spot. He indeed was **foreordained before the foundation of the***

world*, but was manifest in these last times for you*" (1 Pet. 1:18–20).

Some verses strongly indicate, and I firmly believe (though I do not know whether it can be proved from the Scriptures), that God determined *all* of His purposes and all of what would occur in His creation before He brought *anything* into existence. For example, the NKJV (which used the Textus Receptus Greek text) translates Acts 15:18, "*Known to God from eternity are **all** His works.*"

Conversely, the alternative appears untenable. For if that were not the case, then at the time He made the heavens and the earth, He would have had *some* of the details planned out and an *idea* of what His purposes were, but the remaining details and purposes He would need to think through as events unfold—as if He could not be certain what would please Him until He saw and experienced some of what He created. It would be as if He intended to take the first steps, and then see where He would like to go from there—as He learns from His experience and is made wiser. Then also, it would be possible that some of His latter purposes and choices would be constrained because of earlier events and choices which had already occurred and could not be undone or redone—as if He might wish He had understood the ramifications of some earlier choices better.

No, in order for God to know that in the end He would be fully satisfied with all that He had created from the beginning, He would need to know the end from the beginning. As Yogi Berra once quipped, "If you don't know where you are going, you might wind up someplace else."[21] It appears the only way for all that God created to fully satisfy all of His purposes in creation is for Him to have planned and ordained all things together before creation.

A number of passages in Isaiah 41–46 indicate that God has previously determined, and consequently knows, all of what will take place in the future. Indeed, those passages also indicate that His do-

---

[21] Houston Mitchell, Yogi Berra dies at 90: Here are some of his greatest quotes (2015-05-12). *Los Angeles Times*. Retrieved February 4, 2025, from https://www.latimes.com/sports/sportsnow/la-sp-sn-yogi-berra-turns-90-quotes-20150512-story.html

ing so is fundamental to *who He is* as God—and therefore *shows* that He is God. For instance, in Isaiah 41:23–24 and 46:9–11, God says,

> *Show the things that are to come hereafter, that we may know that **you** are gods; yes, do good or do evil, that we may be dismayed and see it together. Indeed you are nothing, and your work is nothing; ... I am God, and there is no other; I am God, and there is none like Me, **declaring the end from the beginning**, and from ancient times things that are not yet done, saying, "My counsel shall stand, and **I will do all My pleasure**," ... Indeed I have spoken it; I will also bring it to pass. **I have purposed it; I will also do it**."*

Here are some similar passages from those chapters:

> *Who has planned and done it, calling forth the generations **from the beginning**? I [the LORD].* (Isa. 41:4 LITV)

> *Who has declared from the beginning, that we may know? And former times, that we may say, "He is righteous"? Surely there is no one who shows, surely there is no one who declares, surely there is no one who hears your words.* (Isa. 41:26)

> *I am the LORD, that is My name ... Behold, the former things have come to pass, and new things I declare; before they spring forth I tell you of them.* (Isa. 42:8–9)

> *Let all the nations be gathered together, and let the people be assembled. Who among them can declare this, and show us former things? Let them bring out their witnesses, that they may be justified; or let them hear and say, "It is truth." "You are My witnesses," says the LORD, "... Before Me there was no God formed, nor shall there be after Me."* (Isa. 43:9–10)

> *Behold, I will do a new thing, now it shall spring forth; shall you not know it?* (Isa. 43:19)

Thus says the LORD, ... the LORD of hosts: "I am the First and I am the Last; besides Me there is no God. And who can proclaim as I do? Then let him declare it and set it in order for Me, since I appointed the ancient people. And the things that are coming and shall come, let them show these to them. ... Have I not told you from that time, and declared it? You are My witnesses. Is there a God besides Me? Indeed there is no other." (Isa. 44:6–8)

I am the LORD, who makes all things, who stretches out the heavens all alone, who spreads abroad the earth by Myself; who frustrates the signs of the babblers, and drives diviners mad; who turns wise men backward, and makes their knowledge foolishness; who confirms the word of His servant, and performs the counsel of His messengers. (Isa. 44:24–26)

In the book of Isaiah, God named the Gentile king—Cyrus—who would command Jerusalem and the temple to be rebuilt. Isaiah wrote that prophecy not only before Cyrus was born, but at a time when Jerusalem and the first temple had not yet been destroyed. We read that prophecy in Isaiah 44:28–45:6:

*Who says of Cyrus, "He is My shepherd, and he shall perform all My pleasure, saying to Jerusalem, 'You shall be built,' and to the temple, 'Your foundation shall be laid.'" Thus says the LORD to His anointed, to Cyrus, whose right hand I have held—to subdue nations before him ... "I will go before you and ... break in pieces the gates of bronze and cut the bars of iron ... that you may know that I, the LORD, who **call you by your name**, am the God of Israel. For Jacob My servant's sake, and Israel My elect, **I have even called you by your name**; I have **named you**, though you have not known Me. I am the LORD, and there is no other; there is no God besides Me. I will gird you, though you have not known Me, **that they may know** from the rising of the sun to its setting that there is none besides Me. I am the LORD, and there is no other."*

Chapter 9

The Paradox

*Do you think that I am **not able** now to call on My Father, and He will place beside Me more than twelve legions of angels?*
—Matthew 26:53 LITV

9.1 God Has Predestined

Given that God has predestined all that we will do and all that will take place in His creation, some wonder what choices we can really have, and what difference our choices—or prayers—could possibly make. That thinking may also lead to a despairing, fatalistic outlook.

That kind of thinking may have been a reason the high priest Eli did not repent and seek mercy when God told him of the judgment He would bring on his house. Instead, he chose to make himself a bad example for us, written for our warning, when he simply said, "*It is the LORD. Let Him do what seems good to Him*" (1 Sam. 3:18). And so, God did.

9.2 We Make Real Choices

As previously described, we have the ability to make choices according to our will, those choices make a difference to what happens, and God rightly holds us accountable for them. Paradoxically, the Scriptures show that we can still have a genuine **ability** to choose something that God has ordained we will not choose—including choices that would be contrary to what is written in His Word! It is a paradox in the sense that God, in His wisdom, has made two things exist together that we might have thought of as mutually exclusive.

Predestination and Our Will

We are given a principal example of this when the Bible tells us that Jesus was given authority in the matter of laying down His life to be crucified for our sins.[22] Jesus said, "*I am the good shepherd ... and I lay down My life for the sheep. ... I lay it down on My own initiative. I have authority to lay it down*" (John 10:14–15, 18 NASB). In Matthew, Jesus told us that He was **able** to prevent people from crucifying Him, and what His Father would do **if** He chose not to lay down His life: "*Or do you think that I am not **able** now to call on My Father, and He will place beside Me more than twelve legions of angels?*" (Matt. 26:53 LITV)

Because that was the case, we can see it was Jesus' *willing* choice to lay down His life. And if that were not the case, how could it have been that "***He offered up Himself***" (Heb. 7:27; see also Heb. 10:12) a sacrifice for the sheep?

Jesus' willing obedience—even to the point of death on the cross—made that obedience especially pleasing to His Father. For Jesus told us in John 10:17, "*For **this** reason the Father loves Me, because **I lay down My life***" (NASB). Note that He did not say, "because He takes My life" or "because He forces Me to lay down My life." Nor would we expect that the Father's *forcing* someone to do anything would, of itself, be a *reason* for Him to love that person.[23]

The Father gave Jesus both the **authority** and **ability** to choose not to be crucified for our sins, **even though** it is written that we were redeemed "*with the precious blood of Christ*" who "*indeed was foreordained before the foundation of the world*" (1 Pet. 1:19–20), and the Scriptures said "*that it **must** happen thus*" (Matt. 26:54). If the Father had not given Jesus that ability, how could it have been

---

[22] Since Jesus is more than a man—being also God—some may question whether this example shows that God would give mere men the same authority to choose something contrary to what He has ordained. Pilate is given as a confirming example later in this section. Personally, I believe that Jesus' example shows us that both God and men can have that ability, and section 9.3 explains *how* each could be true.

[23] It is interesting to observe that, in a sense, *all* who would come after Jesus need to willingly lay down their lives, "*For whoever **desires** to save his life will lose it*" (Luke 9:24).

that Jesus freely chose to lay down His life for us?

It is certain that Jesus would never have chosen **not** to lay down His life for the sheep. One reason being because of His character, and one aspect of that character being that He always prefers to do His Father's will above all else (Luke 22:42; John 6:38; 8:29; 5:30).

Similarly, as described in chapter 7, Pilate was given **power** to crucify or release Jesus. When Pilate was questioning Jesus, he asked, *"Do You not know that I have power to crucify You, and power to release You?"* (John 19:10) Jesus did not correct Pilate. Rather, His answer implied that God *had* given Pilate power to take either action: *"You could have no power at all against Me unless it had been given you from above"* (v. 11).

9.3 How Both Can Be True

We have seen that God has predestined all that we do and all that takes place in His creation. Yet we have the ability to freely make choices according to our will, including some choices that would be contrary to what is written in the Bible, and those choices make a difference to what happens. We do not need to struggle with **whether** these paradoxical truths are both true together. We know they are because *"God, who cannot lie,"* (Titus 1:2) has shown us they are in the written word of God. Nevertheless, it would be helpful to understand **how** that could be the case.

One understanding is based on what is commonly called God's *omniscience*: As 1 John 3:20 says, *"God ... knows **all** things."* Job 37:16 describes God as the One *"who is **perfect** in knowledge."* Psalm 147:5 tells us, *"His understanding is **infinite**."* Isaiah 40:28 says it another way: *"His understanding is **unsearchable**."* These last two verses tell us there is no limit to God's understanding. Therefore, if we were to *search* to find a limit by asking, "But does He know **this**?" it must always be answered **"Yes."**

We might have expected that there is no limit to God's understanding of the creatures and things He has created, for there is nothing about them that He did not make. So perhaps the most awesome aspect of God's omniscience is that He must thoroughly and completely know *Himself*.

Because of that knowledge, God will never be surprised by how He feels about something He has predestined when it comes to pass in the course of time (such as Jesus' crucifixion), nor how He will continue to feel about something as time goes on. It cannot be that God would say, "I did not know I would feel like this!"

It seems this is the only way that He could be faithful to, and not change His mind about, all that He has determined and promised will happen. He will never discover that He is not as pleased (or, as angry) as He thought He would be, or becomes bored, with something He has ordained. He will never cease to love someone whom He determined to set His love upon forever.

It is interesting to consider a situation in which something God has predestined requires that *He* take some action, perhaps even an action that has been prophesied in the Bible. Since "*the Scripture cannot be broken*" (John 10:35), someone might ask whether God has made Himself a **puppet** in His creation **because of predestination**. Does He, or must He, just follow the ordained script?

Asked more articulately, is God **not free** to do according to His will at the time some situation occurs because He is bound to do what He has predestined?

We know instinctively that must not be the case. I do not know of any accounts or teaching in the Scriptures that describe God as being bound by something He has predestined in such a manner that He cannot do His will. Observe also that the general tenor of the Bible's accounts is that God does or will do something because of reasons that **presently** incline His will toward that action. When God takes an action, He does according to what He pleases to do *at the time* He takes the action. As Psalm 135:6 says, "*Whatever the LORD **pleases** He **does**, in heaven and in earth, in the seas and in all deep places.*"

Yet, paradoxically, God has set that truth alongside this one: When God takes an action in a situation, He does what He had predestined He would do. We can see both truths together in God's statement that He declares *"the end from the beginning, and from ancient times things that are not yet done, saying, 'My counsel shall **stand** [it will not be **changed**, but **will** come to pass], **and** I will do all My pleasure'"* (Isa. 46:10).

What has been predestined has not taken away God's ability to **have** a will in His creation, nor to **freely** make choices according to His will. For example, even though the Scriptures had to be fulfilled which said the Christ would be crucified for our sins (Matt. 26:54), we saw in the previous section that Jesus was **able** to choose not to be crucified. Further, He confirmed His ability to *make* that choice by telling us that if He chose **not** to, His Father would place beside Him more than twelve legions of angels to **keep** Him from being crucified (Matt. 26:53). It is astonishing to think of!

How can we understand this paradox? One way is built on two underpinnings.

First, because of His exhaustive knowledge of Himself, God knows what He would prefer (would be His will) to do in any situation—the answer to, "But does He know **this**?" is "**Yes**." It is easy to see *how* God could know what He would choose in any situation since 1) He thoroughly and completely knows Himself, 2) He always acts consistently with His excellent character, and 3) that character never changes. As we would expect of our perfect God, He tells us, *"I am the L*ORD*, I do not change"* (Mal. 3:6), and also *"Jesus Christ is the same yesterday, today, and **forever**"* (Heb. 13:8).

Second, what He has predestined **perfectly fits** what He knew His will would be when each ordained situation arises. In the example above, what He predestined fit Jesus freely choosing to be crucified. Although God **knows** what His choices will be in every ordained situation, He still **freely makes** those choices when the situation occurs. The mere fact that God knows what His willing choices will be does nothing to **constrain** or **change** those choices. It does nothing to make those choices **less real** or **less willing**.

Therefore, God does not need to "**follow** the ordained script" in order to do what it requires of Him at any point in time. When He does what **He pleases** to do in each situation, it "**results in** the ordained script."

Our case is similar. God fully knows us, and as He knows what His will would be in any situation, so He also knows exactly what we would each choose in any situation. God's ability to **predict** our choices in a situation does nothing of itself to **restrict** what we may choose. It does nothing **to us** or our choices that make them any less real or less willing, or to make us less responsible for them.

Each **event** God predestined perfectly fits what He foreknew our choices would be. Note well that we are **not** talking here about **why** God chose to make everything in His creation such that the **script** of **all events** He has predestined would result. We will discuss that in chapter 13, "Why Did God Create All Things?"

These observations enable us to better understand the paradox that we (as also God) can be free to make choices in spite of our actions being predestined. What God has predestined does not take away our **ability** to **have** a will nor to **freely** make choices according to our will. Instead, what He has predestined **perfectly fits** what He knows our choices will be when each ordained situation arises (with its attendant circumstances which may act to constrain, modify, or overrule what our will might otherwise be).

However, there is a "cart before the horse" issue with thinking that God's determination of **what** to predestine was **influenced by** knowing what we would choose. Chapter 12, "Why Did God Make Us Differ?" discusses that issue. Briefly, God more than merely **foreknows** what any person (or creature, or angel) He might create would choose in any circumstance. He exercised complete authority in determining beforehand the numbers and characteristics of all vessels He would **create** and **destine** for different uses. In doing so, He predestined our making and molding, together with all ordained events and circumstances, in order that all that comes to pass, including what we freely choose, fulfills the good purposes of His will—and without any compromise.

In this way, all things work to accomplish God's purposes according

The Paradox

to His will. Those good purposes are not thwarted in the least degree, but rather advanced, by the wills of those whom He has created, no matter how unruly or wicked they may choose to be. As it is written, "*'Why did the nations rage, and the people plot vain things? The kings of the earth took their stand, and the rulers were gathered together against the* LORD *and against His Christ.' ... to do* **whatever** *Your hand and Your purpose determined before to be done*" (Acts 4:25–26, 28).

As we find described in a plain reading of the words in the Bible, we have an ability to freely make choices according to our will and those choices make a difference, yet our good and just God determines all that happens. Think about it. It is both amazing and wonderful that these two aspects of our lives can both be true **together**! As the expression goes, "It is the best of both worlds."

Importantly, we also have the ability to choose to entreat our God for His mercy and help so that we may be given it, even as Jesus "*offered up prayers and supplications, with vehement cries and tears to Him who was able to save Him from death, and* **was heard because of** *His godly fear*" (Heb. 5:7). The Lord told Hezekiah through the prophet Isaiah, "**Because** *you have prayed to Me against Sennacherib king of Assyria,* **I have heard**" (2 Kings 19:20). As it is written, "*The effective, fervent prayer of a righteous man* **avails much**" (James 5:16).

The account in 1 Samuel 23:7–13 provides examples of all these aspects of our lives in God's creation. During a time when Saul was trying to kill David, Saul was told David had gone to Keilah, and he called together an army to go and take David. David heard of Saul's plan and asked God if Saul would come down, "*And the* LORD *said, 'He will come down'*" (v. 11). Then David asked whether the men of Keilah would give him up to Saul, "*And the* LORD *said, 'They will deliver you'*" (v. 12). "*So David and his men ... arose and departed from Keilah,*" and "*it was told Saul ... so he halted the expedition*" (v.13).

David entreated the Lord for help, and he was given it. Knowing from God that he would be delivered to Saul if he stayed in Keilah, he chose to depart. And through all these things, God accomplished His good purposes toward His servant David—to deliver him from his unrighteous enemy. Through this account, God also showed us that He knows what an entire city—composed of many people in various positions of authority and with various capacities to influence—would ultimately decide in a hypothetical situation.

We see that we are able to choose as we will, those choices make a difference to what happens, and it is right to hold us accountable for our willing choices. We also see that we may entreat God for some need or other help, and by doing so may incline Him to give us what we might not have otherwise received (James 4:2b). We can rejoice to know that everything that comes to pass is all of and only what our good, loving, merciful, and just God has **determined** to happen before the foundation of the world. Yet every event that occurs **also** perfectly fulfills God's purposes **at that moment** in the context of all that has happened and we have done.

9.4 How God Can Foreknow Our Choices

As described in the previous section, God's omniscience dictates that He knows with certainty what our choices would be in any circumstance. Were that not so, then—contrary to the Scriptures—there would be a limit to His knowledge and He would not know all things. Nevertheless, it can be helpful to understand *how* He can foreknow what we will choose.

In trying to understand how, we presuppose here that our preference in any given situation is jointly determined by all relevant, existing factors involved. In other words, our will in a situation is formed—and in that sense, caused—by the influence of all relevant factors working together. Prominent among those factors are aspects of ourselves—such as how we have been made, our character and past experiences, our various interests and motives, and our relationships with other individuals who may be involved.

It appears that this presupposition is compatible with the Scriptures, and it does not cause any trouble for other issues and views described elsewhere in this book. Further, our experience is that we

The Paradox

have reasons and motives for our choices, and that we may discover such reasons for other's choices. Almost always, and especially when it comes to the salient factors affecting important choices, our choices are not determined arbitrarily or whimsically.

Nevertheless, we ourselves struggle at times to discern what our preference may be. But in our struggles, we know relatively little about ourselves. For instance, we do not know exactly how our physical brain has recorded our experiences and been affected by them, nor how our brain interacts with our (spiritual and incorporeal) heart, soul, and spirit when struggling to determine what we prefer. We do not even know why and how some thoughts arise in our mind, such as how a solution to a problem might suddenly occur to us ("Eureka!").

By contrast, there is nothing that God does **not** know about each of us, nor about all of the **circumstances** in any situation we find ourselves. In every situation, there is nothing that God did not make or is not aware of. "*He **fashions** their hearts individually; He considers all their works*" (Ps. 33:15) and "*there is no creature hidden from His **sight**, but all things are naked and open to the eyes of Him to whom we must give account*" (Heb. 4:13). The Bible tells us in the preceding verse, Hebrews 4:12, that God not only knows our *thoughts*, but also our heart's *intentions*. Though it is possible we may not fully or accurately understand our own intentions, it is impossible for God not to discern them—for "***all things** are naked and open*" to His eyes.

God knows every electron in every atom in every molecule in our bodies—at every moment its position and velocity and all of the forces acting on it. At a much higher level, He knows each neuron in our brain, and fully knows its operation: when and under which circumstances and how it is activated and functions. He knows how each memory has been recorded, how it may affect our will, whether it is forgotten, and what, if anything, would cause us to remember it.

Thus, even though we may struggle for a time to arrive at our choice, we can see how God could predict the entire process, and what the final result will be. Even in those cases where we might eventually throw up our hands and decide to settle the matter by flipping a coin or casting a lot, we are told, "*The lot is cast into the lap, but its every decision is from the LORD*" (Prov. 16:33).

Chapter 10

How Ordained Events Come to Pass

*His own iniquities entrap the wicked man, and
he is caught in the cords of his sin.*
—Proverbs 5:22

It is helpful to consider what the Scriptures show are some means by which the events God has ordained are brought to pass. How is it that He, as we read in Isaiah 45:7, "*make[s] peace and create[s] calamity*"? How does "*the* LORD, *do all these things*"? In a nutshell, they are brought to pass through the means of both His and our willing choices in the face of various ordained circumstances, together with both natural occurrences and consequences, and God's occasional, supernatural interventions.

Of course, we are not aware of many things at work "behind the scenes." As creatures, our view of what God works to bring things to pass is extremely limited. For example, when we feel hungry, we provide for our body's need by eating food. When we have eaten enough that we are no longer hungry, we imagine we have satisfied that need. But that is only the beginning of an incredibly complex process that God designed to enable our bodies to actively extract nourishment from that food and distribute it to all the cells of the body. Though our own bodies carry out that process, we have very little conscious involvement in it.

10.1 Natural versus Supernatural Means
God uses both natural and supernatural means in bringing about what He has ordained. The Bible talks about "*miracles, wonders, and*

signs" (Acts 2:22; see also Acts 15:12) which God may perform in the heavens and earth. In doing so, it makes a distinction between those "**supernatural**" events (in which God directly intervenes in the ordinary course of affairs to bring about whatever He wants in a way that we would never expect, or is "impossible") and those events that are "**natural**."

God is both faithful (Deut. 7:9) and never changes (Mal. 3:6; Heb. 13:8). He has written the Scriptures to us with commands, statutes, precepts, and testimonies by which He normally instructs and governs us.[24] Those words of God themselves, likewise, also stand faithfully (Matt. 24:35; Ps. 111:7b–9; 119:89–90, 138, 144, 152). They do not evolve nor change, because the God who gave them to us does not change His mind nor eventually come up with a better idea nor learn something new that changes His preference.

In a manner similar to the faithful *Scriptures* God has given to govern us, He has created a physical universe which is "naturally" governed by various *physical laws*. Because He has done so, our experience is that we can see or discover *reasons* for things that happen. That experience is both the motivation and basis for the field of study we call *science*.

It is not our experience or expectation that things happen randomly. We do not wonder what will happen when we lift a ball and let go of it. Although God is *able* to make the sun go back in the sky (Isa. 38:7–8), or to have it stand still in the sky for a day (Josh. 10:12–14), or to darken it (Luke 23:44–45), we have "no doubt" that the sun will rise and set tomorrow, and at precisely predictable times, as it "always" has. And we can explain "why" that will happen.

It appears that God has similarly put in place "natural" laws or mechanisms concerning the *immaterial*. An example might be the effects forgiveness has on the one who forgives. An article on *Johns Hopkins Medicine* website states, "Studies have found that the act of

---

[24] Of course, in the unusual and rare case, God may "step in" to directly give a unique, personal charge to someone—like commanding Abraham to offer up Isaac.

forgiveness can reap huge rewards for your health, lowering the risk of heart attack; improving cholesterol levels and sleep; and reducing pain, blood pressure, and levels of anxiety, depression and stress."[25] God could directly intervene and supernaturally cause all of those health effects in a person who has forgiven another because that pleases Him. But it is not hard for us to imagine our brains being made in such a way that they operate differently when harboring unforgiveness, and that operation affects our bodies. That could be one of myriads of natural mechanisms God has put in place concerning the immaterial (which, in this case, affects also the physical).

This passage from Proverbs seems to describe such a state of affairs, "*His **own iniquities** entrap the wicked man, and he is caught in **the cords of his sin** ... in the greatness of **his folly** he shall go astray*" (Prov. 5:22–23). There is no mention in these particular verses of God intervening in the course of affairs to directly bring judgment on the wicked man. Rather it talks about the consequences that will come from "*the cords of his sin.*" He will be caught in those cords which he was not able to see, and entrapped, and put in a situation which he did not expect and does not desire. Proverbs 11:5–6 also appears to indicate the same: "*The wicked will fall by his own wickedness. The righteousness of the upright will deliver them.*"

Similarly, Proverbs 6:27–35 talks about the consequences which will come upon a man who commits adultery: "*He who does so **destroys his own soul**. Wounds and dishonor he will get, and his reproach will not be wiped away*" (Prov. 6:32–33). It likens the certainty of those penalties to that which occurs naturally due to physical laws: "*Can a man take fire to his bosom, and his clothes not be burned?*" (Prov. 6:27)

Even in the absence of immaterial laws naturally producing consequences for various kinds of behavior, God could naturally bring about those same consequences by ordaining events following that behavior which would produce them. For example, He could use

---

[25] Forgiveness: Your Health Depends on It (2024). *Johns Hopkins Medicine*. Retrieved September 5, 2024, from https://www.hopkinsmedicine.org/health/wellness-and-prevention/forgiveness-your-health-depends-on-it

natural means to uncover one's sin.

At least from what we can observe, and from the results of people's investigations into various events and calamities, it *appears* that God does not *ordinarily* intervene and overrule what would occur "naturally" in what He has created. Perhaps that explains how it is that God *"rested on the seventh day from all His work"* (Gen. 2:2),[26] and yet on the seventh day, all of God's creation "kept going"—His creatures continued to live and move and interact with one another.

10.2 God's Natural Wonders
This state of affairs is a demonstration of God's unfathomable wisdom: It appears He normally *"works all things according to the counsel of His will"* (Eph. 1:11)—to the smallest detail of what occurs in the heavens and the earth—**through,** not **in spite of**, both the natural laws that He has created to govern things together with our natural wills and willing choices (as they may be influenced by the many things described in chapter 3 and the circumstances He has ordained).

God asks in Job 38:22–23, *"Have you entered the treasury of snow, or have you **seen** the treasury of hail, which I have **reserved** for the time of trouble?"* This question strongly implies something which would be an incredible aspect of God's creation, yet it is just the sort of thing we would expect given the situation described above. The context of the passage indicates it is something which should humble us and strike us with awe and wonder at God's wisdom.

The question implies that the way God has created and set in motion the physical universe is such that, in the course of the natural laws He has put in place working themselves out, snow and hail will be brought forth at appointed times to cause some ordained trouble! It is in that sense, I believe, that He described a *"treasury,"* or storehouse, of snow and hail that He has *"reserved"* to carry out His purposes. His description also indicates our utter inability to understand or figure out exactly how He has stored up that snow and hail, and

---

[26] Not in the sense that God was tired and needed rest, but only that He ceased from His work in His creation.

when they will come forth to accomplish His will.

If a hailstorm appointed to bring some ordained trouble is always something God directly and supernaturally causes to happen at the time He desires it, there would be no reserved treasury of hail, nor should our inability to see that treasury humble us. Instead, the rhetorical question might be, "Can you make hail like I can?"

God has given us a small picture and demonstration of this state of affairs by creating us to *begin* as a *single cell* that contains the entire blueprint and all of the physical and biological mechanisms to self-assemble into an adult human being. That assembly must work at the molecular level, and grow into a body that has trillions of cells with various specialized functions and coordinated interactions with other cells. During the entire assembly process—through all of its intermediate states—the unborn child must be able to continue living. For instance, something of a heart needs to be formed and begin beating in the embryo around three weeks after conception (and must not be necessary before then).

The average adult body has about 60,000 **miles** of blood vessels that distribute nutrients to cells in the body's tissues and organs while also carrying away waste products. Those blood vessels need to be created molecule by molecule, and all arranged and distributed in a very particular way to successfully fulfill their role throughout the entire body. Yet the *plan* and *mechanisms* that govern those innumerable, minute actions that will culminate in a fully-grown adult are all in place at the beginning—in that initial, single cell!

Some examples we have seen of God working out His purposes through our natural wills and willing choices were the Jews threatening to accuse Pilate of being against Caesar, and four hundred of Ahab's (false) prophets telling him to go to war against Ramoth Gilead because the Lord would give him success.

10.3 God's Required Intervention

Jesus described an important and universal exception to God's working through natural means when He said, "*No one can come to Me unless the Father who sent Me draws him*" (John 6:44; see also

Matt. 19:25–26, John 15:16, Matt. 11:25, and Mark 3:13). This verse plainly says that it is *impossible* for a man to come to Jesus *without* the Father drawing him. Psalm 65:4 hints at this teaching when it says, *"Blessed is the man You choose, and cause to approach You, that he may dwell in Your courts."*

The sense we get from John 6:44 is that the Father needs to directly intervene to cause things to happen in His creation that will enable or cause a man to willingly do what he would not otherwise. In fact, Strong's *Greek Dictionary of the New Testament* defines the Greek word rendered *"draws"* (Strong's #1670) as "to **drag** (lit. or fig.) [emphasis added]."[27] It is the word used in John 21:11 to describe Peter *dragging* the net of fish to land.

We read earlier Jesus' description of such a direct intervention which, if the Father provided it, *would have* enabled some to repent (though they perished in unrepentance without it): If the miraculous works done in Chorazin and Bethsaida had been done in Tyre and Sidon, *"they would have repented"* (Matt. 11:21). We also read earlier of a case in which God told of His direct intervention to enable a woman to be saved: *"The Lord opened her [Lydia's] heart to heed the things [the gospel] spoken by Paul"* (Acts 16:14). There is no indication Lydia was aware of God's intervention in this way. Then there is Thomas, who understood that he would not be able to believe without personally seeing Jesus raised from the dead, and God granted that to him (John 20:25, 29).

---

[27] James Strong, *Dictionary of the Greek Testament* (New York, NY: The Methodist Book Concern, 1890), 27. It is reprinted (among many other places) in *Strong's Exhaustive Concordance* (Grand Rapids, MI: Baker Book House, 1989, ISBN 0-8010-8108-4).

Chapter 11

Salvation and Predestination

*Therefore I endure all things for the sake of the elect,
that they also may obtain the salvation which is in Christ Jesus.*
—2 Timothy 2:10

God has provided for the forgiveness of our sins and our salvation through the sacrifice of His Son, Jesus Christ. He has told us in the Scriptures what He requires of anyone and everyone to be saved: We must believe in the Lord Jesus Christ (John 3:16; Acts 16:31; John 8:24), repenting from our sins (Acts 2:38; Luke 13:5; Acts 20:21).[28] Note well that the Scriptures distinguish both faith and repentance from works since, properly understood, these are matters of the heart (and for repentance, also the will), not of our deeds.[29]

Since God has predestined *all* things that happen, He has predestined the *subset* of all events that occur in a particular individual's life. And the events that occur in an individual's life include the subset of events, if any, related to that person's salvation. Therefore, as with everything, it is also predestined who will be saved (Eph. 1:4–5; Prov. 16:4; Rom. 8:29–30; 9:22–23).

In an allegory, the narrow gate that leads to life has a sign over it that reads, "Whosoever will may come" (per Rev. 22:17 KJV). But when one who has entered that gate looks back at it from the other side,

---

[28] For detailed, biblical descriptions of saving faith and repentance, see Daudelin, *Repentance and Grace*, chapter 3.

[29] Daudelin, *Repentance and Grace*, 69.

there is a sign over it saying, "Chosen in Christ before the foundation of the world" (per Eph. 1:4).[30]

However, each person's salvation will be worked out in accordance with what God has said is *necessary* to be saved: Those predestined to salvation must be saved through their personal faith (*"For you are all sons of God through faith in Christ Jesus,"* Gal. 3:26). Said another way, Jesus would not save those predestined to salvation if they remained unbelieving (which, in actuality, they will not since *"all that the Father gives Me will come to Me,"* John 6:37).

At the top of this chapter, we read that Paul said, *"Therefore I endure all things for the sake of the elect, **that they also may obtain** the salvation which is in Christ Jesus"* (2 Tim. 2:10). In this verse, *"the elect"* refers to those individuals who will obtain salvation. This raises the question: If they are predestined to obtain salvation, why does Paul need to do anything in order that they *may* obtain it?

What God has ordained is different from **how** it comes to pass. Those whom He has predestined to be saved, He also makes and molds, and brings various events, interventions, and circumstances into their lives such that they ultimately believe and repent.

Jesus described how we must come to Him in Luke 9:23–25:

> *If anyone desires to come after Me, let him deny himself, and take up his cross daily, and follow Me. For whoever desires to save his life will lose it, but whoever loses his life for My sake will save it. For what profit is it to a man if he gains the whole world, and is himself destroyed or lost?*

By definition, for a man to *willingly choose* to come to Jesus, his will needs to be persuaded or changed to *prefer* coming to Jesus over not coming to Him. It is fitting then that fully two thirds of the above passage is devoted to persuading people that coming to Him is their

---

[30] This allegory is loosely taken from remarks attributed to the late Donald Barnhouse found in Philip Ryken's *The Message of Salvation* (Downers Grove, IL: InterVarsity Press, 2002, ISBN 978-0-8308-2404-5), 68–69.

best choice—no matter what the consequences might be to their short life in this world.

It is clear that in order to desire coming to Jesus as Luke 9:23–25 describes, one must believe in Him.[31] Romans 10:14 explains that obvious condition by way of a rhetorical question. It asks, *"How then shall they call on Him in whom they have not believed?"* It similarly explains that in order to believe in Him, one must hear of Him: *"And how shall they believe in Him of whom they have not heard?"*

Accordingly, preaching the gospel is described as a **persuading** in eight separate places in Acts. One of those places is Acts 28:23: *"He explained and solemnly testified of the kingdom of God, **persuading them** concerning Jesus from both the Law of Moses and the Prophets."* The other places are Acts 13:43, 17:4, 18:4, 13, 19:8, 26, and 26:28. Paul described his preaching as **pleading** and **imploring**: *"We are ambassadors for Christ, as though God were pleading through us: we implore you on Christ's behalf, be reconciled to God"* (2 Cor. 5:20).

We can come to believe something through seeking to know the truth. Jesus encouraged people to seek with persistence because those who seek will find (Luke 11:5–10, 13).

The Jews at the synagogue in Berea where Paul preached for a time were seeking. They *"**searched** the Scriptures daily to **find out** whether these things [Paul preached] were so. **Therefore** many of them believed"* (Acts 17:11–12). The Gentile Cornelius was seeking God, and therefore, as he was praying, an angel of God came in a vision

---

[31] We see here that must be a belief which motivates repentance since we are taught a man must *"deny himself"* and *"follow Me* [Jesus]*"* and *"whoever desires to save his life will lose it"* (Luke 9:23–24). A man who *"desires to save his life"* is someone who is not willing to give up some aspect(s) of his life in this world which he understands *must* be given up in order to obey God. That is, he is unrepentant. In a similar teaching in John 12:25, Jesus made explicit He was speaking about one's short life in this world, and whether one's life is lost or kept for eternal life afterward: *"He who loves his life will lose it, and he who hates his **life in this world** will keep it for **eternal life**."*

and said to him, "*Your prayers and your alms have come up for a memorial before God. Now send men to Joppa, and send for Simon whose surname is Peter. He is lodging with Simon, a tanner, whose house is by the sea. He will tell you what you must do*" (Acts 10:4–6). And when the apostle Peter came and preached the gospel to him, he believed and was given the Holy Spirit (Acts 10:44, 47; 11:17).

To summarize, although God has predestined who will be forgiven and saved, their salvation will be accomplished through the means He has said are necessary for Him to save a person. One must hear the gospel, believe in Jesus, and come to Him. That is why it is necessary to preach the gospel to the unbelieving, and encourage them to seek the Lord—so that their hearts and wills may be persuaded. No one will call on Jesus who has not believed in Him, and no one can believe in Jesus without hearing of Him. Accordingly, God's predestining of some to be saved *included* ordaining their making and molding, and the bringing of various events, circumstances, and interventions into their lives such that their personal hearts and wills would be persuaded, at some actual point in time, to believe and repent.

Chapter 12

Why Did God Make Us Differ?

For who makes you differ?
—1 Corinthians 4:7

Consider the question, "Why did God choose some people for...?" Some might answer it, "Not for any foreseen thing in them," and others, "Because He foreknew they would...."

The passage in Romans 9:11–12 has been interpreted to show that the reason God chose Esau to serve Jacob was independent of anything foreseen in either of them. It says, *"(for the children not yet being born, nor having done any good or evil, that the purpose of God according to election might stand, not of works but of Him who calls), it was said to her [Rebecca], 'The older shall serve the younger.'"* This passage tells us that God elected—or chose—Esau to serve Jacob before they had been born or done anything good or evil. It is given as an additional example to the one in verse 9, *"At this time I will come and Sarah shall have a son."* Both passages show that God has chosen beforehand what will happen to fulfill His purposes, and what He has chosen will certainly come to pass.

However, although the account teaches that God chose Esau to serve Jacob before they were born (even as He ordained Jeremiah to be a prophet before he was born, Jer. 1:5), it does not say anything about **why** He chose that.

Further, we know that God also chose to make Esau differ from Jacob. He made and molded the twins Esau and Jacob to have various and different characteristics. For example, *"When her days were fulfilled for her to give birth, ... the first came out red. He was like a hairy garment all over; so they called his name Esau. ... And Esau was a skillful hunter, a man of the field; but Jacob was a mild man, dwelling in tents"* (Gen. 25:24–25, 27). And in Hebrews 12:14, 16–17, we see that one reason God made Esau such that he would act as he did was to *warn* us not to follow his example, considering the consequences.

Wait, are there consequences to being like Esau? If not, then why the warning?

Pondering the question, "Why did God choose some people for…?" is like trying to read half of a torn letter. It presupposes people—prompting one to look for answers with the wrong premise that God has merely chosen among foreknown persons.

However, both the people and their individual characteristics are also **part** of what God altogether chose to create. The way the question is framed hampers us from considering the full authority and control God exerted over **all** His plans for creation—including the characteristics (and numbers) of the vessels that He would make and prepare to fulfill His purposes.

The proper question is, "Why did God **create** some people for…?"[32]

God tells us, *"Everyone who is called by My name, ... I have **created** for My glory; I have **formed** him, yes, I have **made** him"* (Isa.43:7). When we are told that *"God has chosen the foolish things of the world to put to shame the wise"* (1 Cor. 1:27), that should not be interpreted to mean that out of all the people He foreknew, He chose more of the foolish ones to be saved. It means that He chose to **make** more vessels for salvation **to be** the foolish things of the world, and a purpose He had for doing so was to put to shame the wise.

As the potter does, so God also exercises complete authority over

---

[32] This question is addressed in the next chapter, "Why Did God Create All Things?"

making the vessels He has appointed for different uses (Rom. 9:20–21). God makes and molds, and brings into various circumstances, one person differently from another person in order to fulfill all His purposes. For example, He determined to raise up a particularly egregious sinner named Saul (Paul), a blasphemer and a persecutor of God's people, who would eventually believe and be saved as a testimony to other sinners of God's longsuffering—so that they might likewise turn (1 Tim. 1:13, 15–16).

As the potter prepares vessels differently, so that they are suited to the different uses he has planned for each, so God also makes us differ (1 Cor. 4:7)—some are wiser, some stronger, some richer. The Bible teaches us that we have nothing that God did not give us, so we should not boast or be puffed up over others as if we did not receive it (1 Cor. 4:7; John 3:27). What do you think, can a man whom God has made taller than other men rightly boast about his height? Accordingly, God admonishes us, *"Let not the wise man glory in his wisdom, let not the mighty man glory in his might, nor let the rich man glory in his riches"* (Jer. 9:23).

Rather, let a man consider how God desires him to use his talents to serve the One who made him and gave him those talents.

> *For the kingdom of heaven is like a man traveling to a far country, who called his own servants and delivered his goods to them. And to one he gave five talents, to another two, and to another one, to each according to his own ability; and immediately he went on a journey. ... After a long time the lord of those servants came and settled accounts with them. ... His lord said to him [the first], "Well done, good and faithful servant; you were faithful over a few things, I will make you ruler over many things. Enter into the joy of your lord." ... His lord said to him [the second], "Well done, good and faithful servant; you have been faithful over a few things, I will make you ruler over many things. Enter into the joy of your lord." ... And [to the third servant, who hid his talent, his lord said] cast the unprofitable servant into the outer darkness. There will be weeping and gnashing of teeth."* (Matt. 25:14–15, 19, 21, 23, 30)

12.1 Did He Not Make All Differences?

God asks in Isaiah, *"Shall the thing made say of him who made it, 'He did not make me'?"* (Isa. 29:16) Of course, the answer is "It should not be!"

Romans 9:19–21 addresses a different situation: the case of a man who understands that God has made him the way he is, but knowing that God will judge him for what he does, complains to God, *"Why have you made me like this?"* (Rom. 9:20) God's answer in the verse that follows implicitly acknowledges that He did make him like that: *"Does not the potter have authority over the clay?"* (Rom. 9:21 LITV) Section 14.5 will address the man's objection that it is unjust for God to judge him for doing what God had ordained he would do.

In the parable quoted from Matthew 25, the only talents each servant had to work with were the ones they were given by their lord. Accordingly, John 3:27 teaches us that God has given us everything we have: *"A man can receive **nothing** unless it has been given to him from heaven."*

Believers truly differ from one another in both talents and gifts, strengths and weaknesses. Further, it is not wrong (and can be helpful) to discern those differences (for example, see Rom. 12:6–8).

But 1 Corinthians 4:6 expresses our Lord's desire that no one become arrogant, or puffed up, or boast against another regarding something in which they differ: *"that none of you may be puffed up on behalf of one against the other."* Therefore, the next verse rhetorically asks, *"**For** who [inflected as singular] makes you differ?"*[33] Then, there is one who makes us differ, and the obvious

---

[33] The four Greek words of this question may be literally rendered, *"For who distinguishes you?"* The Greek word rendered *"distinguishes"* is the same one that is used similarly in Acts 15:9—which itself may be literally rendered, *"And distinguished nothing between both us and them."* Both of these renderings are essentially identical to that found in the literal, interlinear translations of those verses by Alfred Marshall in *NASB-NIV Parallel New Testament in Greek and English* (Grand Rapids, MI: Regency Reference Library, an imprint of Zondervan Publishing House, 1986, ISBN 0-310-34670-3), 487, 390.

answer is, "God alone." That verse follows up with two more rhetorical questions addressing the same issue: *"And what do you have that you did not receive? Now if you did indeed receive it, why do you boast as if you had not received it?"*

12.2 Some Say He Did Not

Notwithstanding all of the above Scriptures, there are those who postulate (in various ways) a contrary view that people have *some* differing, distinguishing attributes which exist independently of anything God did or has power to do in creating and molding us. In their view, if God were to make two people identical in every way that He is able, *and* were to make all of their experiences and circumstances perfectly identical, those two people could behave differently in identical situations.

Ones who promote such a view should have one or more **reasons** for postulating it. An example reason would be to address a perceived inadequacy or contradiction of the Scriptures in the views described here. They should also have **explanations** for the passages discussed here that appear to **exclude** their contrary view, as well as have passages which **support** their view. They should be able to explain **where** those attributes that exist independently of anything God did or has power to do **come from,** and **how** they exist or come into being.

The view described here is based on the biblical foundation that God, **alone**, has created all things in the universe, together with all their attributes. Further, we have seen that God determined beforehand all that would occur in His creation, including every evil act, so that everything which occurs advances some good purpose(s) of God. The Bible also tells us that God never does what is morally evil. We who believe what the Scriptures teach know that *somehow* these things are altogether true. Chapter 14 explains how that could be.

Chapter 13

Why Did God Create All Things?

*Wanting to show His wrath
and to make His power known, ...
and that He might make known the riches of His glory.*
—Romans 9:22–23

God more than simply *foreknows* what any person (or creature, or angel) He might create would willingly choose in any circumstance. He makes and molds us and ordains all events and circumstances such that all that comes to pass, including what we willingly choose, fulfills the good purposes of His will. God "*works **all things** according to the counsel of **His will**"* (Eph. 1:11), saying, "*I am God, and there is no other; I am God, ... saying, 'My counsel shall stand'*" (Isa. 46:9–10).

Before God created anything, He was alone. By creating these things, He certainly did not make it worse for Himself. We know it must be, at least in the end, "very good." If it were worse, then He would not have done it—He would have just existed alone. Further, it is plain that it cannot be that He has made a mistake that He now regrets, for in that case He would simply annihilate this present creation: "*For You created all things, and **by Your will they** [continue to] exist*" (Rev. 4:11).

Then we can say, "It is good that God is not alone." Similarly, God made a wife for Adam because it was not good for Adam (who was created in His image) to be alone (Gen. 2:18). Through His creation, God has provided a bride for Himself (Eph. 5:25–26, 31–32; Rev

21:2). To provide a suitable bride—washed in Jesus' blood and water so as to be without spot or blemish (John 19:34; Eph. 5:25–27)—Christ's side was pierced (as Adam's side was opened in forming Eve).

When we consider *why* God made the heavens and the earth, we are considering God's *purposes* for doing so. We are told one specific purpose in Romans 9:22, *"God, wanting to show His wrath...."* He wanted to show (manifest, express, or work out) His wrath. It is evident that some other attributes God desired to show are those which Jonah described when He had mercy on the Ninevites: *"For I know that You are a gracious and merciful God, slow to anger and abundant in lovingkindness, One who relents from doing harm"* (Jonah 4:2).

One prominent purpose for God's creation was so that He could work out certain of His attributes—such as mercy, justice, and grace—in ways that He would not otherwise be able to do. For instance, our righteous *"God, wanting to show His wrath,"* could **not** show His wrath without there being people **deserving** of wrath. Similarly, He could not show mercy without there being people in need of mercy. Romans 9:22–23 explains those particular purposes God had in creating us:

> *What if God, wanting to* **show His wrath** *and to* **make His power known**, *endured with much longsuffering the vessels of wrath prepared for destruction,* **and** *that He might* **make known the riches of His glory** *["the glory of His grace" (Eph. 1:6)]* **on the vessels of mercy**, *which He had prepared beforehand for glory?*

In order to accomplish *those* purposes, He needed to prepare both vessels for wrath and vessels for mercy. As it is written, *"the LORD has made* **all** *for Himself [to fulfill His purposes], yes,* **even** *the wicked for the day of doom"* (Prov. 16:4). However, note well that God does not *"have any pleasure at all that the wicked should die,"* but *"that he should turn from his ways and live"* (Ezek. 18:23).

If a person is a great composer, but *never composes anything*, of what value is that greatness? It is in working out that talent that there is glory and fulfillment—in composing a great symphony that a skilled orchestra performs. It is in *hearing* the roll of the timpani, the clash of the cymbals, and the call of the trumpet that the heart is stirred and the composer is fulfilled and his great talent experienced and enjoyed. Regarding this analogy, my wife Vickey made one of her typical incisive observations: "Do people ask a great composer, 'Why have you written music?'"

One of God's greatest attributes is His love (1 John 4:8). And in His creation, He devised an incredible way of working out His great love—taking the form of a man and, bearing our sins, offering Himself a sacrifice, through crucifixion, for those who are unworthy, and doing so even while they were His enemies (Rom. 5:8, 10). This action is held out as the preeminent demonstration of God's love: *"For God so loved the world that He gave His only begotten Son"* (John 3:16).

When God purposed to demonstrate His great love in *that* way, He fully knew the physical and emotional feelings the Father and the Son would experience—the wrath and the suffering and the sorrow. And it happened just as He had before determined (Acts 4:28), and satisfied His purposes completely as He had intended.

Although God has ordained what we do, His emotions associated with our actions were not experienced (at least not fully) when He ordained them, but are experienced when we take them. As we saw in chapter 5, God is pleased and rejoices when we do what is good, and He is grieved and angry when we do what is evil. Of course, whatever emotions our actions might arouse in God, or any other response they may motivate, they are ones that He fully knew and planned in accordance with His purposes in ordaining those events.

For instance, even though Jesus knew that He would shortly raise Lazarus from the dead, when He came and saw his sister's grief, and her weeping over his death, He was also moved to weep: **"When** *Jesus saw her weeping, and the Jews who came with her weeping, He groaned in the spirit and was troubled. And ... Jesus wept"* (John 11:33–35).

Predestination and Our Will

On the sixth day, when God saw all that He had made, it was very good and He was very pleased (Gen. 1:31). But some years later, after sin and death had entered the world, **when** He saw that every intent of the thoughts of man's heart was continually evil, then He was grieved in His heart:

> **Then** *[at that time] the* Lord **saw** *that the wickedness of man was great in the earth, and that every intent of the thoughts of his heart was only evil continually. And the* Lord *was sorry that He had made man on the earth, and He was grieved in His heart. So the* Lord *said, "I will destroy man whom I have created from the face of the earth" ... But Noah found grace in the eyes of the* Lord. (Gen. 6:5–8)

God's grief over what He saw caused Him to rise up and execute a terrible judgment in His wrath upon (almost) all those living on the earth. But this judgment was not an *annihilation* of His creation, as if it had been a *mistake* to make what He did, or as if the result had taken Him by *surprise*.

Instead, this provocation to execute a terrible judgment in the earth was foreordained for His purposes—for one, to work out His wrath against evil, but perhaps also to foreshadow and warn people in all ages of God's dreadful and certain eternal judgment awaiting the impenitent.[34] After the flood, the promised Messiah would still come and at the appointed time as promised—the One who *"was foreordained before the foundation of the world"* (1 Pet. 1:20) and the seed of the woman who would bruise the head of the serpent (Gen. 3:15). The earth with both man and beast continued to exist—unlike what will occur on the coming day of judgment, which has also been foreordained, when the heavens and the earth will be burned up and replaced by new heavens and a new earth (2 Pet. 3:7, 10, 13).

---

[34] I think it also serves to show us that if God truly felt at any time it *was* a mistake to have made this creation, He could have annihilated it.

Chapter 14

God Is Not Evil

*God cannot be tempted by evil,
nor does He Himself tempt anyone.*
—James 1:13

We are taught in 1 John 1:5 that there is no evil in God at all: "*God is light and in Him is no darkness **at all**.*" Not only is God not evil, but James 1:13 (quoted above) tells us He is so thoroughly and completely holy in His nature, that He is not *able* to be *tempted* by evil.

14.1 Why Then Did God Ordain Evil?

People ask, "If God has purposefully created a world in which evil is done, and in fact has ordained every evil act that occurs, is there unrighteousness with God?" We know the Bible answers any such proposed conclusion: "*Certainly not!*" (Rom. 9:14) But many who do not believe in the God of the Bible think that conundrum proves there **could not** be a God who has created this world, or at least not a God who "*is good*" (Mark 10:18), "*almighty*" (Gen. 17:1), and "*worthy to be praised*" (Ps. 18:3).

Naturally, if possible, we would like to understand why our holy God ordained evil, and how it is that He does not share in the unrighteousness of that evil. This section briefly explains some reasons, and summarizes them in a final paragraph. Subsequent sections in this chapter expound upon them.

Contrary to what someone might imply by the above question, God did **not** create a world in which evil is done because He **enjoys** evil.

It is quite the opposite. As described in chapter 13, a reason He created it was to work out His hatred of evil and His wrath against it (Rom. 9:22)—which could not be done apart from the presence of evil.

We saw in chapter 13 that there are other reasons God created this world. Perhaps of more importance was to work out His mercy and love (Rom. 9:23)—since we see on the cross that great mercy and love triumphing over His judgment of evil. His extraordinary mercy and love could not be worked out apart from the existence of vessels who are in need of mercy and unworthy of love.

Further, what God brought into being was *"very good"* (Gen. 1:31). Even Satan was *"the seal of perfection, full of **wisdom** and perfect in **beauty**. ... Perfect in ... [his] **ways** from the day ... [he was] created, till iniquity was found in [him]"* (Ezek. 28:12, 15). Then, it is important to observe the **way** that evil later entered the world.

God has made us such that we have a will and can make choices that we are morally responsible for—and He is not. It appears that evil had its **beginning** in creation when Satan sinned in his heart, as God explained in *"a **lamentation** ... 'Your heart was lifted up because of your beauty; **you corrupted** your wisdom for the sake of your splendor'"* (Ezek. 28:12, 17). Recall that chapter 7 described how it appears we have peculiar ownership of our **own heart's thoughts**—even though God understands all of them. As it is written, *"The preparations of the heart **belong to man**"* (Prov. 16:1).[35] Accordingly, the passage from Ezekiel does not say that iniquity was **put into** Satan's heart, but **found in** him. **He** corrupted his wisdom because of his splendor.

---

[35] I have not found any place in the Bible that describes God as ordaining, determining, [pre]destining, appointing, or even foreknowing our thoughts. Therefore, I do not think it is proper to use any of those words in describing God's relationship to the thoughts and intentions of our hearts. The words the Bible uses are that He *knows* (Matt. 9:4), *understands* (Ps. 139:2; 1 Chron. 28:9), and is *a discerner of* (Heb. 4:12) all the thoughts and intentions of our hearts. Perhaps, in that sense, we might be able to say (with the intended "distance" between God's doings and our thoughts) He can *predict* the thoughts of our hearts.

Satan then deceived Eve by persuading her to believe that **God** had lied to her, and **he** was telling the truth. We saw in chapter 7 that we can do nothing in the world apart from God's will to permit and enable it. But we must place that understanding beside Jesus' teaching that "*whenever he [Satan] speaks a lie, he speaks from **his own** [corrupted] nature, for he is a liar and **the father of lies**"* (John 8:44 NASB). So then, it is **not God** who is the father of (the one who begot) lies, but Satan. In fact, by His nature, "*God ... **cannot** lie*" (Titus 1:2).

We might have expected that God does not sin when He permits someone to speak a lie (like He permitted Satan to lie to Eve). This situation seems somewhat akin to the U.S. Constitution's "free speech" provision. Under it, we do not consider the provision of free speech morally responsible for the lies that are spoken, but liars.[36]

It may be harder to see that when God permits and enables someone to do some cruel and evil thing to another that He has ordained to occur, He does not share in the evil of *that* sin. This state of affairs can be understood as follows: *We* may sin by wrongfully taking what is not ours, and when that occurs, *God has also taken it* (Job 1:21–22). However, *God* does not sin by doing so. For it is plain that there is *nothing* in this world God could take that He did not first give. And He will eventually take almost all things in this corrupted world at some time anyway—including even our lives and the present heavens and earth that have been defiled by sin.

Note that giving people time to repent necessitates allowing them to go on sinning for a time (2 Pet. 3:3–4, 9). Also, we are told that

---

[36] As an aside, be aware that not every lie is sinful (Josh. 2:3–6; 6:17; 2 Sam. 17:18–20). There is significant confusion about this, and someone may object, "What about the Ninth Commandment?" Even as not every killing is "*murder*" (Deut. 5:17; forbidden by the Sixth Commandment), so also not every lie is to "*bear false witness against your neighbor*" (Deut. 5:20). For instance, just as David's servants did not sin when they fought against and killed Absalom's servants (2 Sam. 18:7), neither did the woman sin when she hid Jonathan and Ahimaaz in a well and lied to Absalom's servants who were hunting them (2 Sam. 17:18–20). It would be strange if *killing* Absalom's servants was lawful, but *lying* to them was not.

God's kindness and longsuffering toward those who are evil and unthankful leads them to repentance (Rom. 2:4).

It is because sin and death have entered the world (through Adam's sin, Rom. 5:12) that all suffering and battles exist in this world. But we should put those hardships in a proper perspective. *"All have sinned and fall short of the glory of God"* (Rom. 3:23) and *"the wages of sin [what we have earned] is death"* (Rom. 6:23). Death in that verse refers to the second death—eternal torment in the lake of fire (Rev. 20:14–15). Therefore, all who live on the earth, whatever their circumstances, must say, *"I have sinned, and I have perverted uprightness; and it was not equally repaid to me"* (Job 33:27 LITV).

It is understood in the previous paragraph that "all" does not include the sinless and holy Son of God (who is the only exception). As one of the criminals who was crucified with Jesus testified, *"We receive the due reward of our deeds; but this Man has done nothing wrong"* (Luke 23:41). **His** suffering was for **our** sins, the righteous for the unrighteous (1 Pet. 3:18), bearing our sins in His body on the cross (1 Pet. 2:24). Because of God's great love for us, He sent His Son to die for our sins (John 3:16; Heb. 10:12) so that we can be forgiven.

Finally, those who believe in Jesus are told that *"our light affliction, which is but for a moment, is working for us a far more exceeding and eternal weight of glory"* (2 Cor. 4:17). There will be no sorrow, nor crying, nor pain that the believing and repentant will suffer in the new heavens and earth (Rev. 21:4). As in Jesus' parable, we will enter that eternally blessed state with His commendation and command: *"Well done, good and faithful servant ... Enter into the joy of your lord"* (Matt. 25:21).

To summarize, God did not create a world in which evil is done because He **enjoys** evil. Some reasons were to work out His hatred of evil and wrath against it, and His mercy and love to vessels who are in need of mercy and unworthy of love. It is important to know that what He created was very good, but His creatures corrupted it through sinful choices that we are morally responsible for, and He is not. It is because of that corruption that all suffering exists in this world. God gives people time to repent, which requires allowing them to go on sinning for a time. However, when God permits and enables someone to commit sin, He does not share in its evil. The wages we are due for our sins is eternal torment in the lake of fire. Consequently, all who are living must say they have not been fully repaid for their sins. But Jesus bore our sins in His body on the cross, offering Himself a sacrifice for sins—suffering one of the most excruciating deaths ever invented—so that all who call on Him will be forgiven and live eternally blessed in a new heavens and earth.

14.2 God Never Does What Is Morally Evil

We read this categorical assertion that God will never **do** what is morally evil, nor pervert justice, in the book of Job: "*Therefore listen to me, you men of understanding:* **Far be it** *from God to do wickedness, and from the Almighty to commit iniquity. ...* **Surely** *God will* **never** *do wickedly, nor will the Almighty pervert justice*" (Job 34:10, 12).[37, 38]

It is significant that we find this pronouncement in the book of Job, since that is perhaps the "weakest" platform from which it could be preached. For God first testified of Job, "*There is none like him on the earth, a blameless and upright man, one who fears God and shuns evil*" (Job 1:8). Yet great calamity and suffering were then brought upon him. God permitted Satan to do the cruelest things that he could devise, to Job and all that he had (Job 1:12; 2:6), with the single exception that he could not take his life. As a result, Job would have welcomed death as a mercy (Job 3:20–22; 6:8–9). Also, we have the Scripture's affirmation that it is correct to say that what Job suffered was "*from God*" (Job 2:10; 1:21–22; 2:3).

---

[37] This statement was not spoken by Job, nor one of his three friends (who did not speak what was right about God, as Job 42:7 tells us). It was spoken by Elihu, who spoke the words of God in rebuking Job, saying, "*There are yet words to speak on God's behalf. ... For truly my words are not false; one who is perfect in knowledge is with you*" (Job 36:2, 4).

[38] Be aware that in the Bible, although *evil* commonly refers to what is morally wrong, evil can also refer to something that is hurtful without any suggestion it is morally bad. The latter is the way it is used when it refers to something God has done or may do (for instance, Mic. 2:3 and Ezek. 6:10 [as can be seen in the LITV—which renders Strong's #7451 as "*evil*" in those verses]).

Nevertheless, we will consider a way in which, though there was sin in what was done to Job, God did not share in that sin.

14.3 God Does Not Share in the Evil of Our Sins

In Job 1:14–15, we read of evil that the Sabeans did. They murdered Job's servants and stole Job's oxen and donkeys. They took lives and property that were not theirs. In that same event, God also took those lives and property. However, because He had given them, they were His to take. Indeed, it was *understood* there would come a time when they would be taken. As Job said, *"Naked I came from my mother's womb, and naked shall I return there. The LORD gave, and the LORD has taken away; blessed be the name of the LORD"* (Job 1:21).

We know that Job spoke rightly since the next verse states, *"In all this Job did not sin nor charge God with wrong."* It is not wrong for God to take away what He gave—either things or lives. In fact, as Job recognized, because of Adam's sin (for, *"Through one man sin entered the world, and death through sin,"* Rom. 5:12; see also Gen. 3:19), God will eventually take away each one's life in this world, along with everything one has accumulated in it. As Job said, *"Naked shall I return"* (Job 1:21).

If God can justly take away our *very lives*, He can also justly give us adversity, including taking away our health. Job confirmed this, saying, *"Shall we indeed accept good **from God**, and shall we not accept adversity?"* (Job 2:10) The Scriptures explicitly affirm, *"In all this Job did not sin with his lips"* (Job 2:10).

We recognize that even kings and heads of countries have authority to conscript us into military service and to wage war. And we accept that battlefield commanders have righteous authority to put us into situations where we may lose our health or limbs or lives.

But when *God* does these things, it is always for the good of those who love Him (Rom. 8:28). That includes even our deaths, for *"to depart and be with Christ ... is far better"* (Phil. 1:23; see also 1 Cor. 2:9 and 15:53–57). Thus, the evil which God permitted Satan to do to Job did not result in his destruction, but instead in his sanctification and blessing (Job 42:5–6, 12–15). It was for his good.

14.4 God Does Not Tempt Us to Sin
We are both commanded and taught in James 1:13, *"Let no one say when he is tempted, 'I am being tempted by God'; for God cannot be tempted [literally: 'is untemptable'] by evil, and He Himself does not tempt anyone"* (NASB).

The Greek verb rendered *"tempt[ed]"* here has a few different meanings in the New Testament. When examining this passage in section 3.5, we concluded that it is used here to refer to an internal temptation in which one **seriously considers whether it may be one's will to sin** in a particular way.

God has made us with many desires—as He made Eve with an appetite for food, an appreciation for beauty, and an esteem for wisdom. Since God tempts no one, any desires given by God cannot be inherently sinful by themselves—tempting us to sin—but *"very good"* (Gen. 1:31). However, as we saw with Eve, there may be circumstances in which satisfying their urges would be sinful. And in such circumstances, those desires could become or lead to sinful desires—that do entice and tempt us to sin. In a similar way, *"the love of money is a **root** of **all kinds** of evil"* (1 Tim. 6:10). It led Judas to lie, steal, and betray the Christ unto death (John 12:5–6; Matt. 27:3–4).

The passage in James teaches us that, in analogous circumstances, God would **never** have His desires entice Him to **seriously consider whether it may be His will to sin**. He, and He alone, **is** good: *"No one **is** good but One, that is, God"* (Mark 10:18). By His very nature, God is **untemptable**.

It may be helpful in understanding this aspect of God's nature to consider Jesus' desire not to be crucified, which He expressed to His Father in prayer. He prayed, if possible **and His Father's will**, that cup might pass from Him (Matt. 26:39). It is one thing to desire not to be crucified, and it is both natural and healthy for the flesh to have that desire—even to the point of being *"sorrowful and deeply distressed"* (Matt. 26:37) in anticipation of being crucified. But it is another thing to be carried away and enticed by that desire to **seriously consider** whether it may be one's will **not** to do the Father's will—which Jesus never did, even when facing crucifixion.

Jesus' desire not to be crucified did not entice him to consider choosing not to do His Father's will. Rather, *"when the time had come ... He steadfastly set His face to go to Jerusalem"* (Luke 9:51; see also Isa. 50:6–7).

God's inability to be tempted is given as a reason for something God would never do: *"He Himself does not tempt anyone"* (James 1:13 NASB). Therefore, when someone is being tempted, it is incorrect to say, and one should **never** say, *"I am being tempted **by God**"* (James 1:13 NASB). The kind of temptation the passage in James 1:13–15 speaks of is specifically ascribed to one's own lust—one is carried away and enticed *"by his own lust,"* not *"by God"* (NASB). God's innocence in the face of our own lusts enticing us to sin also appears to be asserted in Ecclesiastes 7:29: *"God made man upright, but they have sought out many schemes."*

Conversely, the Bible shows us that the evil **deeds** which the Sabeans did to Job and others are correctly ascribed not only to the Sabeans, but are also *"from God"* (Job 2:10)—who ordained those events, and permitted and enabled them to occur. But the enticing of the Sabeans to do that evil was not from God, but by their own lusts.

Romans 1:24 tells us that God can give us up to the lusts of our hearts. That is, He can withhold or take away *restraint* that He might otherwise give us. But that is far different from *giving* us sinful lusts.

Matthew Henry's Commentary on the Whole Bible offers the following comments on this passage from James:[39]

> He [God] cannot be a promoter of what is repugnant to his nature [evil]. ... It is very bad to sin; but is much worse, when we have done amiss, to charge it upon God, and say it was owing to him. ... Neither the devil nor any other person or thing is to be blamed so as to excuse ourselves; for the true original [sic; origin?] of evil and temptation is in **our own hearts** [emphasis added].

---

[39] *Matthew Henry's Commentary on the Whole Bible* ([Reprinted] Peabody, MA: Hendrickson Publishers, 1991, ISBN 0-943575-32-X), 2409.

14.5 God Justly Finds Fault with Sinners

Romans 9:19 voices a different (and much lesser) charge against God that the impenitent may raise: that God is unrighteous in *holding them accountable* for their willful sins because they have done only what God predestined and created them to do. For instance, those who willfully crucified the Christ might object to being charged with that heinous sin by complaining they had only done *"whatever Your hand and Your purpose determined before to be done"* (Acts 4:28).

It is in that way that a man complains about being judged for his sins in Romans 9:19, saying, *"Why does He still find fault? For who has resisted His will?"* That impertinent question could be rephrased, "Isn't it unrighteous of God to hold us accountable for our sins given that He has made and molded us and brought us into the circumstances by which He has predestined—'*determined before to be done*'—all that we do?"

Observe that this is a very different question from, "How has God made us *such that* it is right to hold us responsible for the evil we do?" The Bible does not answer that different question in this passage, nor do I know of any other place it is explained. When I think about what the explanation might involve, it seems certain the answer is not something we could comprehend.

There are things which we, as creatures, simply cannot understand—but can only stand in awe of what God has done. Interestingly, the book of Job mentions some of those things:

> *Indeed, can anyone understand the spreading of clouds [and give us infallible weather forecasts]? ... He does great things which we cannot comprehend ... those wondrous works of Him who is perfect in knowledge ... Where were you when I laid the foundations of the earth? ... To what were its foundations fastened? ... Where is the way to the dwelling of light? And darkness, where is its place? ... By what way is light diffused, or the east wind scattered over the earth?* (Job 36:29, 37:5, 16, 38:4, 6, 19, 24)

But this man's impertinent question in Romans 9:19 is answered, in the two verses that follow it, with three rhetorical questions:

1. reproving his brazenness in accusing God of unrighteousness in things he is unable to comprehend,
2. implicitly acknowledging that God has made and molded us such that we do all His will, and
3. unapologetically asserting His righteousness in so making and molding us, and in using His vessels in accordance with the purposes for which He has made them—even as no one would ever accuse a human potter of unrighteousness for doing the same with vessels the potter makes.

The passage is quoted below, with bracketed numbers indicating the three parts of the reply that are outlined above:

> *[1] But indeed, O man, who are you to reply against God? [2] Will the thing formed say to him who formed it, "Why have you made me like this?" [3] Does not the potter have power over the clay, from the same lump to make one vessel for honor and another for dishonor?* (Rom. 9:20–21)

Because the Scriptures directly answer this very question, we do not need to seek other answers. Moreover, other answers may even detract from or distract us from the one that God has given.

Chapter 15

Conclusions

*Oh, the depth of the riches both of the wisdom and knowledge
of God! How unsearchable are His judgments
and His ways past finding out!*
—Romans 11:33

Some of the significant conclusions a careful study of the Scriptures in the preceding chapters has led us to are summarized here. A correct understanding of them, altogether, should encourage and inspire us—indeed, lead us to rejoice and praise God!

15.1 What God Predestined

In God's plans for what He would create, He determined beforehand **all events** that would occur—and everything that He has determined to occur **will** come to pass. Consequently, everything that happens is all of and only what our good, loving, merciful, and just God has ordained to happen.

Because He did so, there is no question that all of His purposes in creation will be accomplished; for every event that happens works to fulfill the purposes He had before the foundation of the world. And when each of those predestined events occurs, it **also** perfectly fulfills God's purposes **at that moment** in the context of all that has happened and we have done, and all that He desires to bring to pass in the future.

15.2 God's Purposes in Creation

Examples of some of God's purposes in creation are to enable Him to work out His great love and mercy on unworthy vessels (Ps. 103:8, 10–11), and His wrath against evil (Rom. 9:22–23)—attributes of God which, if not for creation, would never find expression. His plans for creation included the characteristics and smallest details of the diverse people and everything else He would both make and prepare to participate in bringing about ordained events.

15.3 How Events Are Brought to Pass
Events are brought to pass through the means of both God's and our willing choices in the face of various ordained circumstances, together with both natural occurrences and consequences, and God's occasional, supernatural interventions. However, as all of those things are brought to pass, God never does what is morally evil, "*nor does He Himself tempt anyone*" (James 1:13).

15.4 God's Free Choices
The general tenor of the Bible's accounts is that God does or will do something in a particular situation because of reasons that *presently* incline His will ('Because you did this, I...'). This understanding is behind the prayers in the Bible—with their supplications and reasonings, beseeching God to grant some request (Matt. 15:22–28; Ps. 107).

In every situation that arises in His creation, God freely does what He pleases **at the time** He does it. Nevertheless, those actions are just what He had predestined He would do. That is the case because what God had predestined He would do **perfectly fits** what He infallibly foreknew His feelings and purposes and willing choices would be at the time each situation arises.

In other words, God never finds Himself compelled to take an action that is against His will in order to fulfill what He had ordained before the foundation of the world. He has no need to **"follow** the ordained script" in order to do what it requires of Him at any point in time. Instead, as He does what He pleases to do in each situation, it "**results in** the ordained script."

15.5 Our Free Choices
God has given us the ability to make choices according to our will,

including ones that would be against His will, sinful, or hateful to Him. At least some times He gives us power to freely make choices that would be contrary to what He has *ordained* (or even to what may be *written in His Word*)—as Jesus was able to choose not to be crucified (Matt. 26:53), and Pilate had power to release Him (John 19:10). Our choices make a difference, and God rightly holds us accountable for them.

Accordingly, it is hard to find a page in the Bible that does *not* contain instruction or an example that teaches or tries to **persuade us** to turn from sin or choose what is good because of the various **consequences** we can expect those choices to bring. And we may be justly praised or blamed, punished or rewarded for those choices.

However, what God has ordained in any situation, and therefore has purposed and prepared to occur, is **in accordance with** what He infallibly knows we will choose. Like the potter, God exercised complete authority in determining beforehand the numbers and characteristics of all vessels He would create to fulfill His good purposes. Therefore, those purposes are not thwarted in the least degree, but are instead advanced, by the wills of those whom He has created (Acts 4:26–28).

15.6 How Should I Feel About This?

We see on almost every page of the Bible an affirmation that our natural thoughts about our choices and natural interpretation of our experiences are correct: We are able to choose as we will, those choices make a difference to what happens, and we will rightly be held accountable for our willing choices (as others for theirs). Those truths provide strong motivation to prefer wise choices, and the Bible is full of teaching aimed at persuading us to choose the good and reject what is sinful.

We also see that we may entreat God for some need or other help, and by doing so may incline Him to give us what we may not have otherwise received (James 4:2b). That motivates Christians to offer *"up prayers and supplications, with vehement cries and tears"* (Heb. 5:7).

Yet because of these truths, we might have thought that we—or even God Himself—are subject to the choices and whims of others. We might have thought that it could be God's will to bless us with some good thing, or to do some good work through us, but some person, or country, or even Satan could thwart those plans, and even kill us, through their actions.

If we thought that, then we might have also thought that God can only *intend* to work all things together for good to those who love Him (Rom. 8:28), but believed the actuality to be that He will do the best He can in the face of unpredictable actions by His creatures. And we might be hard-pressed to explain how we can be certain prophecies will come to pass, given such unpredictability.

But we can rejoice to know that those thoughts are not correct. Even though we have a genuine ability to choose according to our will, everything that comes to pass is all of and only what our good, loving, merciful, and just God has **determined** to happen before the foundation of the world. Also, every event that occurs perfectly fulfills God's good purposes **at that moment** in the **context** of all that has happened and **we have done**. Proverbs 26:2 describes something that is an inevitable consequence of this state of affairs—that all events have a purpose or cause: "*A curse without cause shall not alight*" (see also Matt. 10:29 and Amos 3:6).

What God has made is truly astonishing and wonderful—that these profound realities coexist in truth! God "*does* **great** *things, and* **unsearchable**, *marvelous things without number*" (Job 5:9).

Isaiah cries out to us, proclaiming God's power and purposes displayed in His creation:

> "*Behold your God!*" ...
> *He who sits above the circle of the earth, ...*
> *who stretches out the heavens like a curtain ...*
> *Lift up your eyes on high, and see who has created these things,*
> *who brings out their host by number; He calls them all by name,*
> *by the greatness of His might and the strength of His power;*
> *not one is missing.* (Isa. 40:9, 22, 26)

Conclusions

And David extols God's great mercy and love, and His open ear to save those who cry out to Him:

> *Great is the L*ORD*, and greatly to be praised; ...*
> *His greatness is unsearchable. ...*
> *The L*ORD *is gracious and full of compassion,*
> *slow to anger and great in mercy.*
> *The L*ORD *is good to all,*
> *and His tender mercies are over all His works. ...*
> *The L*ORD *is near to all who call upon Him,*
> *to all who call upon Him in truth.*
> *He will fulfill the desire of those who fear Him;*
> *He ... will hear their cry and save them.* (Ps. 145:3, 8–9, 18–19)

Scripture Index

Genesis
1:26–27 18
1:31 .... 22, 24, 82, 84, 89
2:2 66
2:7 15
2:16–17 22
2:18 79
3:4–5 22
3:6 21
3:8–10 22
3:9 28
3:12 23
3:13 35
3:15 82
3:16 35
3:19 88
4:8–10 22
4:9 28
6:5 46
6:5–8 82
6:7 46
8:20–21 37
17:1 83
20:6 46
25:24–25 74
25:27 74
50:20 44

Exodus
3:14 34
8:15 30
8:32 30
9:34 30
10:7 30
11:10 30
12:10 45
14:17 30
32:7–8 37
32:10 37
34:25 45

Numbers
33:4 30

Deuteronomy
5:17 85
5:19 36
5:20 85
7:9 64
16:4 45
32:39 47

Joshua
2:3–6 85
6:17 85
10:12–14 64

1 Samuel
3:18 .... 40, 53
19:19–24 32
19:23–24 26
23:7–13 59
23:11 59
23:12 59
23:13 59

2 Samuel
17:18–20 85
18:7 85

1 Kings
21:19 27
21:21–24 41
21:25 .... 27, 41
21:27 41
21:29 42
22:6 28
22:7–9 28
22:10 27
22:12 28
22:19 28
22:20 .... 27, 28
22:22 29
22:23–29 29
22:34 46

2 Kings
19:20 59
20:1 40
20:5 40

1 Chronicles
5:19–20 40
21:1 26
28:9 .... 42, 84

2 Chronicles
6:8 46
12 39
12:6 39
12:7 39
16:9 42

Ezra
1:1 31

8:22–23 41

Job
1 28
1:6 28
1:7–8 29
1:8 87
1:10–11 28
1:12 87
1:14–15 88
1:21 88
1:21–22 .... 85, 87
2:3 87
2:4–5 23
2:6 87
2:10 .... 87, 88, 90
3:20–22 87
5:9 96
6:8–9 87
12:14 45
33:27 86
34:10 87
34:12 87
36:2 87
36:4 87
36:29 91
37:5 91
37:16 .... 55, 91
38:4 91
38:6 91
38:19 91
38:22–23 66
38:24 91
42:5 9
42:5–6 .... 28, 88
42:6 23
42:7 87
42:12–15 .... 28, 88

Psalms

Reference	Page
18:3	83
19:11	22
22:24	41
33:15	16, 23, 27, 61
51:5	25
65:2	41
65:4	68
94:7–9	22
97:9	28
101:7	27
103:8	94
103:10–11	94
105:17	44
105:25	27
107	94
111:7–9	64
115:2	47
115:3	47
119:59	15
119:67	23
119:89–90	64
119:133	30
119:138	64
119:144	64
119:152	64
135:6	19, 47, 56, 94
139:2	84
139:13	23
139:14	15
139:16	49
145:3	97
145:8–9	97
145:18–19	97
146:4	15
147:5	55

Proverbs

Reference	Page
3:5	22
5:22	63
5:22–23	65
6:27	65
6:27–35	65
6:32–33	65
7:6–27	26
7:21–22	26
11:5–6	65
14:12	22
16:1	46, 48, 84
16:4	69, 80
16:9	43, 46
16:25	22
16:33	46, 62
20:24	46
20:30	23, 30
21:1	27, 28
23:15–16	37
26:2	96
30:6	13
30:8–9	23

Ecclesiastes

Reference	Page
7:29	90
11:9	35, 36

Isaiah

Reference	Page
1:18	16
10	45, 48
10:5	48
10:7	48
10:7–11	48
10:12	48
10:13	48
10:15	48
14:24	47
14:27	47
29:16	76
38:7–8	64

40:9	96
40:22	96
40:26	96
40:28	55
41–46	50
41:4	51
41:23–24	51
41:26	51
42:8–9	51
43:7	74
43:9–10	51
43:19	51
44:6–8	52
44:24–26	52
44:28–45:6	52
45:7	47, 63
46:9–10	47, 48, 79
46:9–11	51
46:10	57
50:6–7	90
53:10	17
66:3–4	36

Jeremiah

1:5	49, 73
9:23	75
10:23	46
18:7–8	41
31:33	32
32:19	37, 39, 42

Lamentations

3:32–33	17
3:37	44

Ezekiel

6:10	87
18:23	80
18:30–31	23
22:31	37
28:12	25, 84
28:15	25, 84
28:17	25, 84
36:26	32
37:3	29

Daniel

4:35	19

Amos

3:6	47, 96

Jonah

3:9	41
3:10	41
4:2	80

Micah

2:3	87

Zechariah

12:1	16, 23

Malachi

3:6	57, 64

Matthew

1:17	49
1:18	24
1:20	24
4:1	25
9:4	84
9:17	32
10:28	15
10:29	47, 96
11:20–22	24
11:21	68
11:21–22	21, 24

Scripture Index

11:25	68
12:43–44	27
12:43–45	27
15:22–28	94
19:4	23
19:25–26	68
24:35	64
25	76
25:14–15	75
25:19	75
25:21	75, 86
25:23	75
25:30	75
25:41	31
25:46	31
26:3–4	44
26:5	44
26:14–16	35
26:37	89
26:39	89
26:53	53, 54, 57, 95
26:54	54, 57
27:3–4	89
27:4	36
27:19	45

Mark

3:13	68
5:2	27
5:5	27
5:15	27
10:18	34, 83, 89
14:11	44

Luke

1:35	24
8:21	12
8:55	15
9:23–24	71
9:23–25	70, 71
9:24	54
9:51	90
11:5–10	71
11:9	33
11:13	71
13:5	69
16:26	31
18:4–5	15
22:21–22	36
22:42	55
23:22	45
23:41	86
23:44–45	64
24:19	28

John

3:3	32
3:14–15	44
3:16	17, 44, 69, 81, 86
3:27	45, 75, 76
5:30	55
6:37	70
6:38	55
6:44	67, 68
7:38–39	32
8:24	69
8:29	55
8:44	25, 29, 85
10:14–15	54
10:17	54
10:18	54
10:35	56
11:33–35	81
11:33–37	17
12:5–6	89
12:6	35
12:25	71
15:16	68

18:27–28	45
18:38	45
19:4	45
19:6	45
19:8	45
19:10	45, 55, 95
19:11	45, 55
19:12	45
19:12–13	45
19:30	15
19:34	80
20:25	68
20:29	68
21:11	68

Acts

2:22	64
2:38	69
4:19	16
4:25–26	59
4:26–28	95
4:28	12, 44, 59, 81, 91
5:3	26
5:3–4	35
5:4–5	35
10:4–6	72
10:44	72
10:47	72
11:17	72
13:43	71
15:9	76
15:12	64
15:18	50
16:14	31, 68
16:31	69
17:4	71
17:11–12	71
18:4	71
18:13	71

19:8	71
19:26	71
20:21	69
26:28	71
28:23	71

Romans

1:20	9
1:24	90
1:28–29	29
2:4	86
2:4–5	31
2:6	37
2:8–11	37
2:14–15	16, 36
3:23	86
5:8	81
5:10	81
5:12	24, 86, 88
5:19	32
6:17	25
6:23	86
8:9	32
8:9–11	27
8:11	32
8:28	28, 47, 88, 96
8:29–30	69
9:9	73
9:11–12	73
9:14	83
9:19	91, 92
9:19–21	76
9:20	76
9:20–21	75, 92
9:21	76
9:22	80, 84
9:22–23	69, 79, 80, 94
9:23	84
10:14	33, 71

Scripture Index

11:33 93
12:6–8 76

1 Corinthians
1:27 74
2:7 12
2:9 88
3:16 27
4:6 76
4:7 .... 73, 75, 76, 77
5:7 44
15:41 16
15:53–57 88
16:12 15

2 Corinthians
4:17 86
5:9 42
5:10 31
5:17 32
5:20 71
9:7 20

Galatians
3:26 70
6:15 32

Ephesians
1 18
1:4 70
1:4–5 .... 11, 12, 69
1:5 .... 12, 18
1:6 80
1:11 .... 18, 19, 47, 66, 79
2:1 25
2:3 25
3:20 9
5:25–26 79
5:25–27 80

5:31–32 79

Philippians
1:23 88
2:13 .... 18, 31, 43

1 Thessalonians
2:3 12
2:13 12

1 Timothy
1:13 75
1:15–16 75
6:10 89

2 Timothy
2:10 .... 69, 70
3:16 .... 12, 13

Titus
1:2 .... 55, 85

Philemon
14 .... 11, 12

Hebrews
2:16 30
4:12 .... 61, 84
4:13 61
5:7 .... 40, 59, 95
7:27 54
8:10 32
9:14 32
10:12 .... 54, 86
10:16 32
10:22 32
12:14 74
12:16–17 74
12:24 32

13:8 .... 57, 64

James
1:13 .... 25, 32, 83, 89, 90, 94
1:13–15 90
1:14 .... 25, 32
1:14–15 25
1:15 26
2:26 15
4:2 .... 40, 60, 95
4:8 41
4:10 41
4:13–16 .... 43, 45
4:15 48
5:16 .... 40, 59

1 Peter
1:6–7 17
1:18–20 50
1:19–20 54
1:20 .... 49, 82
2:24 86
3:18 86

2 Peter
3:3–4 85
3:7 82
3:9 85
3:10 82
3:13 82

1 John
1:5 83
3:20 55
4:8 81

Revelation
2:10 25
4:11 79

20:10 31
20:14–15 86
20:15 31
21:2 80
21:4 86
22:17 69

www.ingramcontent.com/pod-product-compliance
Lightning Source LLC
Chambersburg PA
CBHW060845050426
42453CB00008B/840